GROWING
CACTI
AND OTHER
SUCCULENTS
IN THE
GARDEN

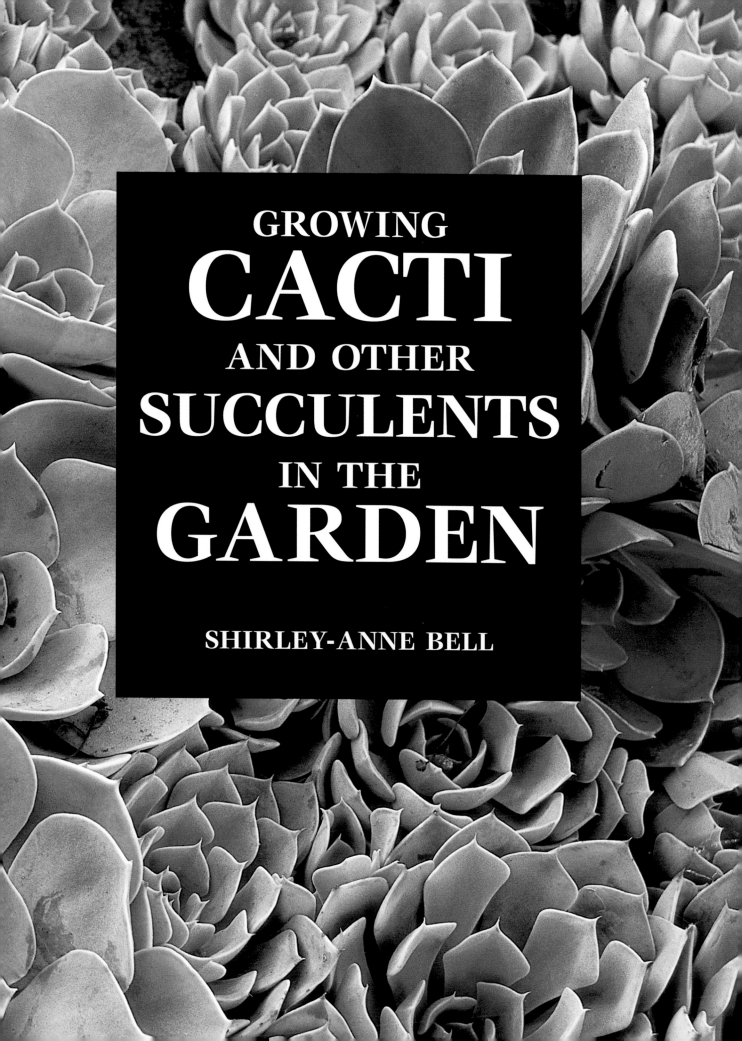

GROWING
CACTI
AND OTHER
SUCCULENTS
IN THE
GARDEN

SHIRLEY-ANNE BELL

First published 2001 by
Guild of Master Craftsman Publications Ltd,
166 High Street, Lewes,
East Sussex BN7 1XU
Copyright © GMC Publications Ltd 2001
Text © Shirley-Anne Bell 2001

ISBN 1 86108 197 9

A catalogue record of this book is available from the British Library.

Editor: Nicola Wright
Designer: Jane Hawkins
Photographer: Neville Bell (except page 135 Vivian Russell, The National Trust, Waddesdon Manor)
Typeface: Veljovic & Geometric
Colour separation: Viscan Graphics (Singapore)
Printed and bound by Kyodo Printing (Singapore)
under the supervision of MRM Graphics,
Winslow, Buckinghamshire, UK

10 9 8 7 6 5 4 3 2 1

Foreword

Like most groups of plants, cacti and succulents go in and out of fashion. Over the last hundred years this cycle has occurred a number of times, the most recent peak in popularity being the 1970s. At that time, exploration of cactus and succulent plant habitats discovered many new species and importation of plants into Europe created a wave of interest.

This interest waned in the 1980s and early 1990s partly as a result of the fuel price increases which made it more expensive to heat greenhouses. The popularity is now again on the increase. One of the reasons for this is the realization that some of these plants will grow outside in Britain, particularly with the right preparation of the site. Many more types can be used for summer bedding creating exotic and spectacular displays for the garden.

This development is being paralleled in other parts of northern Europe and northern USA but each area has its own unique problems. Many cacti and succulents are very cold tolerant experiencing much lower temperatures in their natural habitat than we get in Britain. Our particular problems are the humidity of our winters and lack of winter sun.

This book is therefore particularly timely as it contains unique information for creating such gardens successfully in Britain. It is the result of many years of experimentation by the author, Shirley-Anne Bell. The detailed and practical knowledge of what is possible will, I am sure, create much interest and be an invaluable guide to those looking for something a little different in their garden.

Tony Mace
Publications Manager
British Cactus and Succulent Society

Acknowledgements

I would like to thank my husband, Neville, for all his hard work on the photographs and the help he has given throughout every step of this book, from developing the first ideas, through all the construction work – digging, sawing, humping, building – and finally to the hours of help with checking the names of the plants. I would also like to thank our son, Jon, and, of course, my mum, for all their help in keeping the day to day business running whenever I went AWOL on the book.

Special thanks must go to my editor, Nicola Wright, who has worked on the book with patience and good humour, despite being inundated at times with new pictures, name changes and far too many afterthoughts. I would also like to thank her for helping to bring logic and order into the plant information in Chapter 2 and the Plant Directory. My thanks too to the designer, Jane Hawkins, who has done such a magnificent job of making the book visually exciting.

Last but not least, many, many thanks to the following people who so kindly allowed Neville to take photographs of their premises:

Baytree Garden Centre, Spalding, Lincs., for letting us use pictures of their inspirational container plantings which appear on pages viii, 60, 66, 73, 79, 131, 133, 134 and 150. Mr and Mrs R Oliver of Station Road, Swineshead for letting us illustrate their exotic garden scheme in Chapter 2 and for all their combination planting for Chapter 8 on pages 110, 113, 116, 121, 122, 125 and 144. Tim and Mink Wilson of Plant Lovers' Nursery, Candlesby, Lincs., for some of the species shots on pages 109, 153, 163, 167, 168, 169, 171 and 178. Mr R Smy of Peterborough for allowing us to photograph his hardy cactus gardens for pages 13, 16, 26, 49, 124 and 154. Mrs M Pearson of Abbey Road, Swineshead, pages 56 and 67. Mr and Mrs C Stopper of Pilley's Lane, Boston, pages 107 and 152. Mr and Mrs B Welberry of North End, Swineshead, pages 113, 117 and 120. Mr M Welberry-Smith and Holme Farm Produce (Boston) Ltd, pages 93, 108 and 112. The National Trust at Waddesdon Manor for the picture of their succulent carpet bedding scheme inspired by John Hubbard's landscape painting, featured on page 135.

Naming Plants

Plants are grouped, or classified, according to common characteristics. The names they are given indicate to which group they belong. The largest grouping, based on the structure of the plant's flowers, fruits and other organs, is the family. The family is then divided into genera and the genera into species. Every plant has a botanical name which is composed of two parts, the first indicating its genus and the second its species (written in italics). Species may be further divided into subspecies (subsp.).

Additional names indicate whether the subject is a hybrid (a cross between different genera or species, shown by ×), a cultivar (a man-made variation; the result of breeding, beginning with a capital letter in single quotes), a variety (a naturally occurring variation as opposed to a man-made one, var.) or a form (a plant with only a minor, but generally noticeable variation from the species, f.). Series or groups are collections of hybrid cultivars of like parentage.

Many plants are known by two names, or have been known by another name in the past; to avoid confusion, these names may be given as synonyms (syn.). Common names (colloquial, everyday names) are also used.

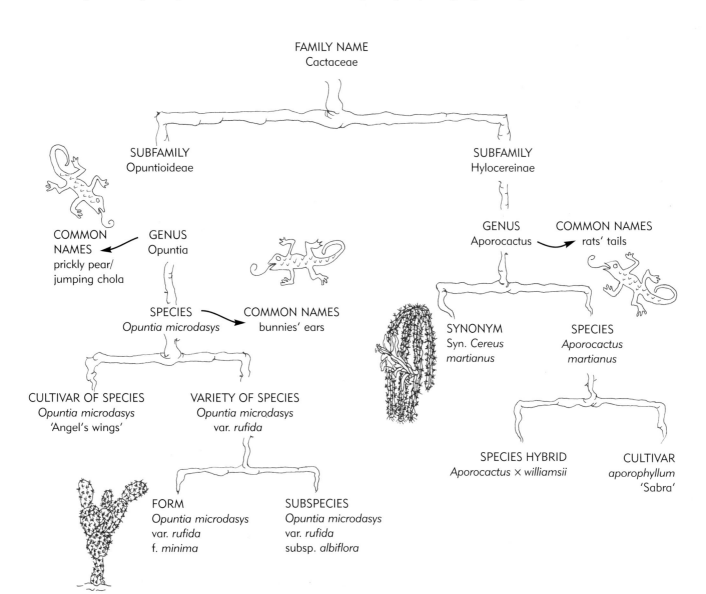

FAMILY NAME
Cactaceae

SUBFAMILY
Opuntioideae

SUBFAMILY
Hylocereinae

COMMON NAMES
prickly pear/
jumping chola

GENUS
Opuntia

GENUS
Aporocactus

COMMON NAMES
rats' tails

SPECIES
Opuntia microdasys

COMMON NAMES
bunnies' ears

SYNONYM
Syn. *Cereus
martianus*

SPECIES
*Aporocactus
martianus*

CULTIVAR OF SPECIES
Opuntia microdasys
'Angel's wings'

VARIETY OF SPECIES
Opuntia microdasys
var. *rufida*

SPECIES HYBRID
Aporocactus × *williamsii*

CULTIVAR
aporophyllum
'Sabra'

FORM
Opuntia microdasys
var. *rufida*
f. *minima*

SUBSPECIES
Opuntia microdasys
var. *rufida*
subsp. *albiflora*

CONTENTS

Introduction
THE GREAT ESCAPE!

Ask most people to picture cacti and succulents and the image that comes to mind can, unfortunately, be a depressing one. Lines of dusty pots in the darker corners of garden centres, supermarkets and other shops. Plants forgotten in houses. They turn up over and over again, either as etiolated specimens, thin and soft, desperately straining towards the light, or desiccated and stunted as they burn up, unfed and unwatered, depending on whether they are on a sunny or shady windowsill.

The drought resistance and tolerance of neglect of cacti and succulents, which are their greatest assets, can also be their downfall. They are very, very hard to kill, so they can linger on almost indefinitely in a dreary Cinderella-like condition. Even when they are well looked after, cacti and succulents are often displayed in rows of pots, like a parade of soldiers. Although they may be a delight to their owner, with their multitude of shapes, sizes and flowers, they can seem just a little dull to the uncommitted onlooker, who does not appreciate the minutiae of their spination, colour and form, or their cunning adaptations to their hostile native habitats.

There are undoubted joys in collecting cacti and succulents. Some people like to assemble a collection of a single genus, with all of its species and subspecies, while some like to collect the rarest specimens, and spend their spare time in an avid hunt for a missing gem. Others like to concentrate on a region and collect the representative plants from, say, Bolivia. Still others love them for the thrill of the miniature, and relish every tiny detail, even down to staining the transparent windows of lithops, or 'living stones', with dye, and examining the cells through a microscope. These plants have a great fascination for the very young, and many collectors start out with a pocket money collection. Conversely, older people, who have had to give up the pleasures of their flower borders and vegetable plots, can still have the joys of gardening in miniature, even if the 'garden' only fills the top of a bedside table near a window.

So this book is not for the seasoned collector, who already loves cacti and succulents and has found a space in his or her life for a collection of them. Instead it is for non-cactophiles. It is for people who like the look of cacti and succulents, and love the idea of using them in novel and exciting ways in their garden. Rather than growing them in the traditional setting of the greenhouse or windowsill (ideally a sunny one), they want to let them break out and take their place as some of the most exciting plants ever to be seen growing in British gardens.

Some of the plants are fully hardy and can stay out all the year round, regardless of what the British climate cares to throw at them. If you are prepared to spend a little more time, an even wider range of planting can be achieved by using cacti and other succulents in half-hardy schemes, where they are bedded out in the warmer months, once the danger of frost is over.

These plants lend themselves to some of the most interesting garden displays you can imagine, in gravel and scree beds, rockeries with a difference, small front gardens, and some of the basement and courtyard gardens and other smaller spaces which are a feature of modern homes. They complement all sorts of hard landscaping, from traditional stone paving, through to timber decking. They create displays that have a more contemporary feel than the traditional, high-maintenance lawns and borders, which often depend on sweeping perspectives for their best effects. The scale of planting can range from their use as striking accent plants in containers around patios and sitting out areas to a total, uncompromising garden makeover with a really radical feel.

Agave americana, left, and *Trachycarpus fortunei*, right, tolerating the worst of winter weather with impunity

Cacti and succulents also associate well with a whole range of other dramatic architectural plants, and will grow happily alongside palms, phormiums, bamboos, ornamental grasses and other spiky subjects.

These schemes are visually very exciting. Because the plants are strong in structure and novel in appearance, they are a great choice for high-impact gardens with eye-catching displays designed to set off your house and environment. They create the maximum impact in the minimum space, so they are an excellent choice for even the

smallest garden, and a lifesaver for those awkward tiny front gardens, or areas alongside drives and entrances which need something to soften the hard landscaping. They also have a contemporary, almost minimalist, appeal, which means that they associate particularly well with the sleek lines of modern architecture.

Most schemes are quite easy to plan and to put into practice and they also have the important advantage of being relatively cheap to set up. Some of the largest plants, like a mature cactus, palm or large bamboo, are undoubtedly expensive. However, these function as accent plants, the exclamation marks in your scheme, and therefore you need relatively few of these. Or, if you have patience you can plan ahead, using

After over-wintering outside, this group of plants is completely unscathed. L to r, *Phormium* 'Yellow Wave', *Agave americana*, *A. americana* 'Variegata', and *Aloe aristata*, with *Echeveria* 'Perle von Nurnberg' in the background

temporary plants as infillers, while the plant you are waiting for establishes itself. A huge pampas grass, for example, makes a showy specimen plant, which you can afford to move out when you need to.

Many of the plants do have the advantage of growing rapidly, and some of the smaller succulents will spread to fill every corner that you will allow them to occupy. So, once you have bought these particular plants, that's it. Wait for them to grow and you can increase them by division.

In the following pages, you will be shown how to plan each area you want to plant up, taking into account your geographical position in the UK and your local conditions. These local conditions relate to the aspect of your garden, whether it is north, south, east or west facing, whether it is sheltered or exposed to wind, and what soil type you have. The use of the plants in all sorts of settings is described – including scree gardens, unusual rockeries, patios and decking, water features and a range of attractive containers. There is advice on how to incorporate these striking new kinds of plants into more traditional gardens and into mixed planting schemes. And for those of you who fancy a living family coat of arms, then carpet bedding schemes, those Victorian must-haves, are also covered.

There is a lot of information on what to look for in the plants and which species to choose. Each chapter also covers types of planting, construction of the garden features you wish to include, and how to prepare the area in which the plants will be growing. The book also describes the best and most dramatic ways to display the plants so that they look good and – most important of all – gives you

the care information to ensure that they stay looking good!

Probably the most tempting thing these planting schemes have to offer is the fact that they are extremely low maintenance and therefore give you more of the most precious commodity of modern day – time. Once cacti, succulents and other architectural plants have been set out, they need far less care and attention than annual bedding schemes, herbaceous borders and kitchen gardens. Traditional gardening is, sadly, very high maintenance and it was easier to manage when, as was often the case in the past, someone tended to be around the house most of the time. A gorgeous herbaceous border, cottage garden and vegetable plot are wonderful additions to anyone's home environment and they give an immense amount of pleasure both to the person who creates them and to those who reap the benefits. But this is if, and only if, your garden is your hobby and this is how you want to spend your time. Otherwise, it can become a source of irritation and pressure in what is probably already an only too hectic life.

So the plants featured here all have the advantage that they fit well into busy lives, when people would much rather treat their garden as an extra outdoor 'room', where they can sit and relax after work, supervise the children at play, and share drinks and barbecues with friends. Sadly, gardening can be a chore, with constant weeding and watering, deadheading and pruning, and traditional plants will seldom tolerate much neglect. These drought-tolerant choices mean that you can choose how much time you want to spend on your plants, and when you want to spend it – instead of the plants dictating their needs to you.

It is this drought resistance which is another of the great advantages of the plants used in the book. Global warming is an established fact, and the hotter, drier summers that have resulted have brought with them a frustrating era of drought and hosepipe bans. 1999 was, with 1990, the joint warmest since records were begun, over 300 years ago. In both years the average temperature for central England was 10.6°C or 51.1°F, and 1999 was globally the fifth warmest year ever recorded.

In April 2000, a conference on the impact on global warming on gardening was told that experts predict that southern England will eventually become more like the South of France climatically, while the north of the country and Scotland will resemble Cornwall. Mike Calnan, Head of Gardens at the National Trust, said that climate change was already altering historical gardens, and New Zealand, South African and Mediterranean species were beginning to be used. He spoke of "climatic conditions which are themselves becoming historic" and predicted that "some of the layouts and plants we have in our collections may no longer be sustainable".

In March 2000, the National Trust, the Royal Horticultural Society and the Government's UK Climate Impacts Programme announced an investigation into how the climate changes may affect the Trust's 200 gardens in England, Wales and Northern Ireland. The Institute of Terrestrial Ecology predicts that spring will come earlier and winters will become increasingly frost free in much of the UK. During the twentieth century, the UK climate warmed by half a degree centigrade, which has reduced the number of days with the temperature below freezing in central England from 15 to 20 in the eighteenth century to 10 days now. And the average

temperature is predicted to rise by between 1 to 3°C (2 to 5°F) during this century.

This means that we haven't seen anything yet! There is already nothing more discouraging than coming home to containers of wilted summer bedding, or, even worse, when water restrictions have been imposed, having to watch your carefully planned borders droop and fade for the sake of a good watering. Cacti and succulents, on the other hand, all take their shapes and forms from their adaptation to living in conditions of drought and erratic water supplies, so they will show no sign of damage during dry spells, though they will, of course, welcome a good soaking when it does come. Now you can go on holiday without wondering what sad casualties you might find on your return!

Cacti and succulents and their companion plants have the benefit that they are also colourful all the year round. Unlike some gardens, which almost disappear during the winter months, the hardy plants carry on bravely through everything the winter months can throw at them. They are evergreen, though green is a misnomer, as they come in a wide range of eye-catching colours, from purples and blacks, through pinks, lilacs and turquoise, to variegated whites, yellows and silvers. If you have a planting of hardy sedums and a mixture of showy phormiums then, even in the dead of winter, you can look out on an attractive display of colours, shapes and textures, and dream of a warmer, brighter, subtropical world.

The half-hardy plants, on the other hand, the succulent 'moveable feasts' of the plant world, can live a wonderful second life during the colder times of the year. By moving them into striking containers, which are now readily available in garden centres and DIY stores at astonishingly low prices, you can utilize the plants in spectacular, indoor displays for the house, conservatory, enclosed porch or garden room. If you don't have anywhere to display the plants, many of them can be kept dry and stored safely over winter in an unheated greenhouse, or even in a garage or shed. Though it is a pity to hide them away.

Last but not least, the plants are flexible and forgiving. They can be used in schemes as big or small as you choose, from a single bed, to a mould-breaking patio, through to the whole garden. They are the perfect answer to awkward areas. They will live happily in containers, which you can move all around the garden for an ever-changing kaleidoscope of effects. Lower growing species will cover steep banks with a weed-suppressing evergreen patchwork, while those tricky pond edges, where the liner will persist in peeping out, can be covered in glorious living carpets of colour and flower.

So, with all these irresistible advantages, what are you waiting for? Let the great escape of cacti and succulents into the wide world of the outdoors begin!

The architectural garden, seen here from above, can make a bold statement with a mixture of container planting and hard landscaping features, including raised beds, patios and decking

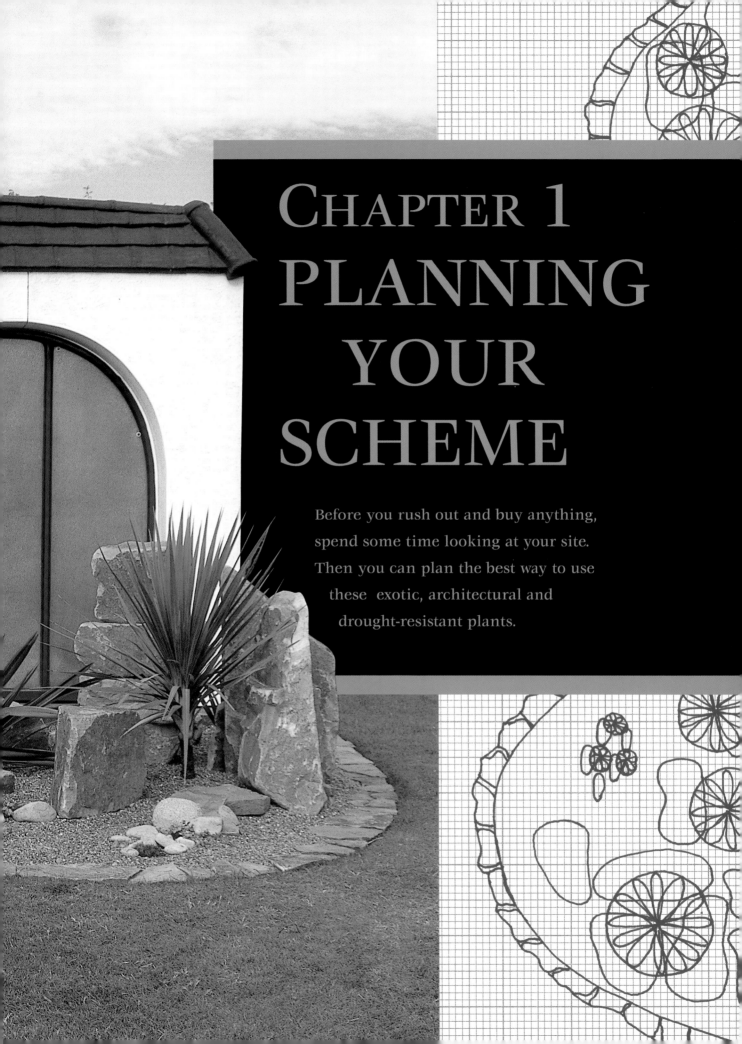

CHAPTER 1
PLANNING YOUR SCHEME

Before you rush out and buy anything,
spend some time looking at your site.
Then you can plan the best way to use
these exotic, architectural and
drought-resistant plants.

This book aims to help you by offering a number of individual approaches to gardening with unusual, drought-resistant and architectural plants. It tackles a variety of sizes and types of scheme, from an individual bed to a total garden makeover.

The first decision, therefore, is one of scale. Take a bit of time here, walking around your plot, examining it from the point of view of visitors, passers by, callers and most importantly of you and your family, who are the main 'consumers' of the scheme.

The second decision, if this is to be one feature of several in a garden, is integration into the existing scheme. These plants lend themselves to smaller scale planting, rather than the big sweep of lawn and trees, so for visibility you may want to consider an area close to the house which can be viewed when you are indoors as well as outdoors. It may be your sitting out area where you entertain friends and watch the children playing. It may be those awkward architectural features close to the house, where the angles of house walls, porches, steps etc. cry out for a more adventurous treatment. In these cases, you need to consider careful demarcation; the concept of garden rooms is a useful one here, where you can move from one area of the garden to another with the judicious use of hard landscaping with paths, low walls, trellis panels etc.

One of the easiest ways to introduce this kind of gardening is to use the front and back of the house as different zones. In this case 'the great escape' can offer the ideal solution to the perennial front garden problem, where size, shape and demands of callers conflict. You need space for car parking and manoeuvring, and also a convenient route for delivery people to reach the house. All this plus easy access for the inhabitants can conflict, with path, drive, lawn and flower beds all competing for their share of an already small space.

A narrow border can be turned into an attractive gravel garden, with a mixture of architectural planting, versatile containers, and strategically placed rocks

If you are looking for one small scheme, dip in and out of the chapters to look for something which offers a solution to your particular problem space, or something which you find particularly exciting and inspiring. There is loads of variety, from scree beds to striking rockeries, from water features to conversation-piece patios with paving and decking – almost anything you can think of, down to just one dramatic container which can easily be moved from spot to spot.

Or, if you are really ambitious, you can use the book to plan your total makeover step by step, and put each step into practice by working your way through the whole book.

Although the temptation is to get started straightaway on the ground, this can be wasteful not only in the monetary sense, but also in terms of time and patience and sheer hard work. Therefore your scheme should be planned as carefully as possible beforehand, which saves on mistakes that can be ugly, unsuitable and expensive, or all three if you are unlucky! Look at the following:

WHAT IS THE SCALE OF THE SCHEME YOU ARE PLANNING?

The first decision is to decide whether you are looking at the design and implementation of an individual feature or if you are embarking upon a full-scale makeover of your whole garden. Whatever the scale of the scheme, it is advisable to plot your site carefully. If you are designing an individual feature, you need to look at the site as a whole to see how it will fit in with existing features. A full-scale redesign should still be broken down into a number of areas and features, which can be planned individually, with integration into a whole borne in mind.

Although it is anathema to many people, it will pay dividends to measure up and plot your garden onto graph paper because it is surprisingly hard to sketch out the propor-tions accurately from memory or by guesswork. This plotting will take two of you unless you are particularly adept with a tape measure. If your site is regular, it is quite easy to pace out, or preferably to measure the dimensions, and transfer them to scale on your graph paper.

In the case of irregular features, you can use triangulation to get the dimensions down on paper. Please don't stop reading here! I saw

maths as 'time out' for daydreaming when I was at school and even I think that it really couldn't be easier.

Step 1 is to find two fixed features that are permanent, say two trees, one washing line post to the other, a shed wall to a fence, or whatever. Measure the distance between these two points, A to B, and transfer this line A–B as a scale measurement to your plan.

Step 2 is to measure the distance from A and then from B to the feature C which you want to locate accurately on your plan. This gives you figures for the length of A–C and B–C. Change these measurements to your scale measurements for the plan.

Step 3. Take a pair of compasses and fix them at the scale measurement of A–C, put the point in at A and draw an arc. Repeat for B–C. C is located where the two arcs intersect on your plan.

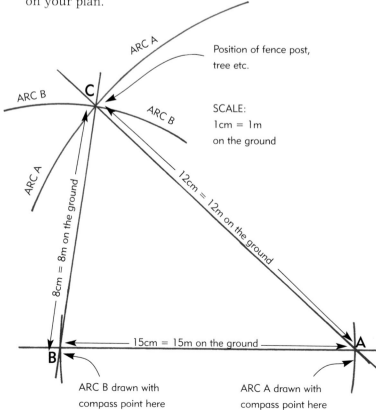

ARC A

Position of fence post, tree etc.

ARC B

C

ARC B

SCALE:
1cm = 1m
on the ground

ARC A

8cm = 8m on the ground

12cm = 12m on the ground

15cm = 15m on the ground

B

A

ARC B drawn with compass point here

ARC A drawn with compass point here

By transferring these measurements to your plan and joining them up you will get the accurate scale dimensions of your site. If you have lots of awkward curves and angles, repeat the triangulation exercise as often as you need to, until you have the shape transferred to your drawing. When you have got your shape marked out, go upstairs and check out of the window to make sure that it looks correct. (A bit like checking your calculator totals roughly in you head, just to make sure that you haven't entered something incorrectly.)

If you really have a maths phobia, can't face the planning and measuring stage, and you are determined to get going, then take a few minutes longer just to go upstairs. An aerial view of sorts can be obtained from looking out of each of your upstairs windows, as it is surprisingly difficult not to lose sight of the overall shape and scale of your garden when you are on the ground.

After you have measured out your site and transferred the measurements, mark out all the major fixed features, like hard landscaping, paths, walls, steps and patios, and larger features you are planning to keep like vegetable plots, borders and mature trees.

If you have access to a photocopier, make several copies that you can then draw onto until you get the scheme you like the best. Alternatively, invest in a big pad of tracing paper so that again, you can try several

Make a scale drawing of your garden feature to help you visualize your scheme. Then sketch in the plants and hard landscaping you would like to use

versions. Whatever you do, keep a basic copy of the plan, because you are almost guaranteed to use it again. However sure you are that your final design really is final, you may be surprised to find the inspiration that can strike you when you are actually out in the garden constructing your scheme. Don't be afraid to modify your plans if inspiration suddenly strikes, or something just doesn't look right. Most people make changes even if they have paid a professional designer.

It is also incredibly useful to take a set of photographs of the site. You can draw your new features onto the pictures with a marker pen so that you can get a three-dimensional impression of how your garden or feature is going to look. Of course, if you can draw you can bypass this step and sketch your dream landscape. And don't forget there are any number of garden design programmes for your computer, although you will still need to get out there with your tape measure and notebook to get the correct dimensions in the first place.

If you are lucky enough to have the budget for a garden designer and/or a landscaping contractor use the guidelines you would for choosing a builder and try to find a personally recommended professional whose work you can take a look at (see Further Information). And make sure that you get on! Some people want someone else to come up with the creative ideas. Other people have an idea of exactly what they want with no room for manoeuvre. So make absolutely certain that whoever you choose understands what you require from them. It's your garden and it should express and realise your dreams – unless they are totally impractical, in which case you should be shown how a version of your fantasy can be brought into existence.

Hardy cacti and succulents look very effective against gravel, cobbles and paving in this unusual border, thriving in a sunny south-facing front garden in Peterborough, East Midlands

WHAT IS THE ASPECT OF YOUR SITE?

Your garden plan gives you the basics of the size and shape of your garden, but other features are also very important and will strongly affect the type of scheme you can have. First of all, add the direction your garden faces to your plan, as these plants need the maximum light and sun, so you need to plan for south or southwest-facing features if possible. Keep your northerly aspects for your shade lovers and mini-woodland corners!

Again you want a well-drained position, unless you are considering a rockery or raised bed, which will automatically give you a garden with drier conditions. Consider how exposed the site is, because a sheltered site gives a much more favourable microclimate for your plants. Look at how much windproofing you have already and what you

might need to add. It is often overlooked factors, like wind damage and a high water table, that take their toll on more tender plants rather than cold as such, so an enormous amount can be done to make their conditions of growth more favourable. For example, lewisias and agaves can both be borderline for hardiness, but will be infinitely more resilient if they are planted in free-draining soil at a 45-degree angle, so that water drains out of the rosettes of leaves. Think of the cliffs in the Spanish Costa Brava resorts like Lloret and Blanes. All those postcards of agaves, silhouetted against the scarlet and gold sunset skies, show them growing at an acute angle, with enormous flower spikes towering above them. Since *Agave americana* is sometimes known as the century plant for its renowned tardiness to flower, the postcard specimens are obviously telling you something about the conditions that they like.

WHERE DO YOU LIVE?

Before splashing out on plant purchases take a good look at your geographical location, both in a broad sense and in the local sense, where factors like a town or open country-side location make a great difference because of the effects of local microclimates in towns and cities.

Raw temperatures are important, of course. But apart from the north/south contrast in temperatures, where much of Scotland, for example, is in a different temperate zone to the rest of the British Isles, look also at your height above sea level, your rainfall levels, and whether you are in a rural or urban setting. As an illustration, although gardens in the southeast may be colder than those in

Half-hardy cacti and succulents make a colourful summer display in this gravel garden planted with *Agave americana*, stripey *A. americana* 'Variegata', the contrasting bright green *Aeonium arboreum* and purple-black *A. arboreum* 'Zwartkop' and the tall column of *Cereus forbesii*

the milder southwest, because the east is drier and sunnier, many plants will thrive which would succumb to the damper, duller conditions in the west. Then there are also purely local features, like being sited in a localized frost pocket, to consider.

As a generalization, then, the low-lying areas south of Newcastle upon Tyne are generally favourable to growing these plants. The southeast of England is particularly favourable, because it is dry and sunny. The southwest is good, too, though because it is much wetter, you may need to look at sloping beds and raised, free-draining beds with added gravel for porosity. Coastal areas are milder, so even as far north as the west coast of Scotland offers wonderful conditions. The temperature is significantly higher in cities so this again improves your scope, as well as idiosyncratic details, like how sheltered you are. Because it is damp, rather than cold, which will kill cacti, succulents and their companions, you may have an advantage if you have an area with an overhanging balcony, say, which will keep plants drier, though the benefits of this protection are cancelled out if the plot is too shady as a result.

In many ways Britain has a very favourable climate, because being an island protects it from large temperature swings. Britain has what is described as a maritime climate, which is one of few real extremes. This distinguishes Britain from regions which have the temperature extremes of a continental climate. As a result, we don't have the very cold winters and very hot summers of much of America and mainland Europe, and this actually gives Britain a wider range of species which do not have to tolerate such huge variations. This, of course, explains the

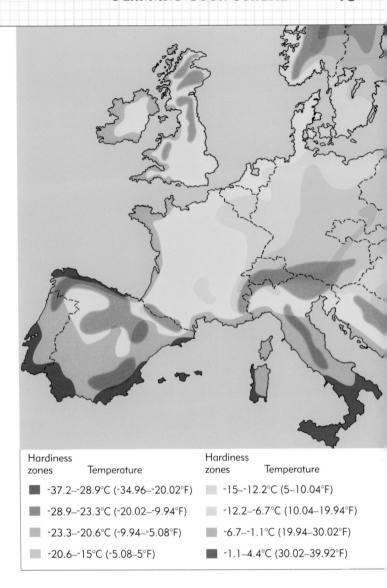

Hardiness zones	Temperature	Hardiness zones	Temperature
■	-37.2–-28.9°C (-34.96–-20.02°F)	■	-15–-12.2°C (5–10.04°F)
■	-28.9–-23.3°C (-20.02–-9.94°F)	■	-12.2–-6.7°C (10.04–19.94°F)
■	-23.3–-20.6°C (-9.94–-5.08°F)	■	-6.7–-1.1°C (19.94–30.02°F)
■	-20.6–-15°C (-5.08–5°F)	■	-1.1–4.4°C (30.02–39.92°F)

municipal gardening policy of say, Annecy, in southeast France, for example. The summer gardens around the city are actually planted with many of the species which you will find in these pages, cannas for flowering centrepieces for example, instead of the more subtropical planting that the deceptively high summer temperatures there might lead one to expect.

For many years the Americans have used the Harvard University-derived system of 'hardiness zones' to judge how plants will grow and which species will thrive. This can be adapted for use in the UK. The map above gives a quick summary of the hardiness zones of Britain and Europe.

This hardy cactus and succulent garden is well protected, growing in a sheltered, southwest-facing position with windbreaks either side and a wall at the back to retain the sun's warmth

HOW MUCH EFFORT ARE YOU PREPARED TO PUT INTO MODIFYING YOUR SITE?

Despite what may appear to be intractable conditions, you can do a lot to modify your particular site to make it more favourable to plants and therefore to expand the range of plants you can use in your scheme.

Windproofing the area to create a sheltered planting feature automatically raises the temperature and protects your plants from wind damage. If you are planning one feature, look for a ready-made sheltered position, like house walls, the right-angle where the garage wall perhaps projects forward from the house, an enclosed patio and so on. You may have existing hedges and fencing; if not, are you prepared to spend time and money on adding these? There are all sorts of possibilities offered by trellis

panels and other ornamental structures, which both divide spaces and act as protection. These features also help to divide up garden features, particularly very dissimilar ones, like an ornamental garden from a vegetable garden, or a wild garden from a formal garden. This also gives a series of 'garden rooms', where the garden is revealed little by little as you move around in it, which can add interest and apparent size. Make sure the resulting space is not too gloomy for the plants, however.

If you have a wall at the back of your feature, this has the advantage of acting like a storage heater, absorbing the heat of the sun and releasing it over a period of time which gives your plants more favourable conditions. You can also consider painting the wall a lighter colour to reflect and maximise the warmth of the sun, though this is difficult to remove if you decide to change things later.

If you have a high water table or your plants have to be at the bottom of a slope, you have the choice of constructing an unusual rockery, or a raised bed to improve drainage. If you don't want a rise in the level, you can also improve the soil by digging in quantities of gravel, laying land drains, or draining the area into a pond.

As mentioned above, it's also important to select the most favourable aspect, e.g. south or southwest facing if possible. In extreme cases you may have to rotate your garden so that your exotic feature is at the furthermost end of your site. For example, you may have to site a feature like a patio or a summer house against a far wall or fence if proximity to the house means that you would otherwise have to set your plants in a cold and shady position.

WHAT SAFETY FACTORS NEED TO BE TAKEN INTO ACCOUNT?

When your plan includes spiky plants, water features, rockeries, raised terraces, steep steps or decking you have to consider who will be using your garden. Although these features can look fabulous they are not necessarily the safest or most user-friendly options. You may have to reconsider if you have young children and/or inquisitive pets. There are also constraints when designing for the elderly, or for those with disabilities, if, for example, you need to make provision for wheelchair access, or handrails on steps and other features.

If you have children or pets, spikes may need to be trimmed off some of the agaves and yuccas, for example, or the plants need to be situated well away from exploratory fingers or noses. Children can drown in quite literally a few centimetres of water, so a pond may need to be put on hold. If you have to have the sight and sound of water there are safe and attractive alternatives, where the water is contained in an underground tank and bubbles up safely through a millstone or out of a water feature onto stones.

Low-maintenance, drought-resistant cacti and succulents are ideal in many ways for the elderly or disabled gardener. Raised beds offer a combination of advantages here, affording ease of access and maintenance for the gardener along with a well-drained position for the plants.

Succulents, like fully hardy *Sedum cauticola 'Lidakense'* and *S. pachyclados*, growing here by the pond-side, make colourful, low-maintenance choices

HOW MUCH TIME DO YOU WANT TO SPEND?

This is one of the crunch questions. In many ways this sort of gardening is far less demanding than the more traditional garden with its annual bedding, its herbaceous borders and its lawn to care for.

If your biggest priority is to save time and effort, then this will largely determine whether you will be opting for a fully hardy planting scheme. If you don't mind spending more time, then consider a mixed scheme which will need attention in the spring and autumn, when half-hardy material is planted out and lifted, and which will need some forethought and planning for over-wintering the more tender plants. Then there is the halfway house where you have a fully hardy permanent planting, plus moveable containers planted with half-hardy subjects which just need moving in and out with the seasons. These give you the added benefit of providing winter colour and interest indoors.

AND HOW MUCH MONEY CAN YOU SPEND?

It is possible to create an instant garden with tall palms, dramatic agaves, and whispering groves of bamboo, but only if you have a bottomless bank balance.

Most gardens, however, mature over time. This, therefore, is another case for taking a good look at your plan of the garden and experimenting, by drawing in various combinations of the plants that will make the strongest architectural statement over time, before you actually purchase anything.

These plants give you a skeleton planting which will take several years to reach maturity; in this case, Chapters 2 and 8 give some idea on faster growing material which will infill while your main planting puts on flesh. This infilling material can then be divided or moved to start another exotic feature.

AN EXAMPLE OF AN EXOTIC GARDEN FROM DESIGN TO COMPLETION

Friends asked me to design an exotic garden feature for them which would enhance the appearance of their swimming pool extension, and this has created an ideal opportunity to describe the stages which go into planning any sort of garden feature.

The illustrated scheme is a design for a 6.5m (21ft 6in) long and 3m (10ft) deep bed to go alongside the south-facing wall of the extension. This extension has arched, translucent panels which can be removed in the summer, so that the pool will sometimes be viewed through the feature.

After measuring the site I sketched two possible schemes, (see drawings on page 12 and opposite); a semicircular bed and an irregularly curved bed, both containing a variety of hardy and half-hardy planting and large rock features. The rock features were intended to curve round to suggest the course of a dry stream bed. We agreed on a low-maintenance scheme, and chose plants that are completely hardy in this part of south Lincolnshire, near the coast in eastern England, where my friends live.

Because the pool house has asymmetrical panels, they preferred the curved design, which we all felt was more sympathetic to the structure. The design projects forwards on the right, which contains a very strong vertical feature, composed of rocks and *Cordyline australis*, which will become a small tree in time. This was included to add weight to the side with the narrower removable panel. A *Trachycarpus fortunei* on the left will balance the scheme as it increases in height. The phormiums and yuccas will give a medium height underplanting. Although *Phormium* 'Sundowner' will become a large subject in

time, a mature clump can be divided to give material for architectural planting elsewhere.

The final scheme was then transferred to graph paper (see plan below).

The swimming pool extension needed an exotic garden feature to enhance its appearance from the outside and the inside when the panels are removed

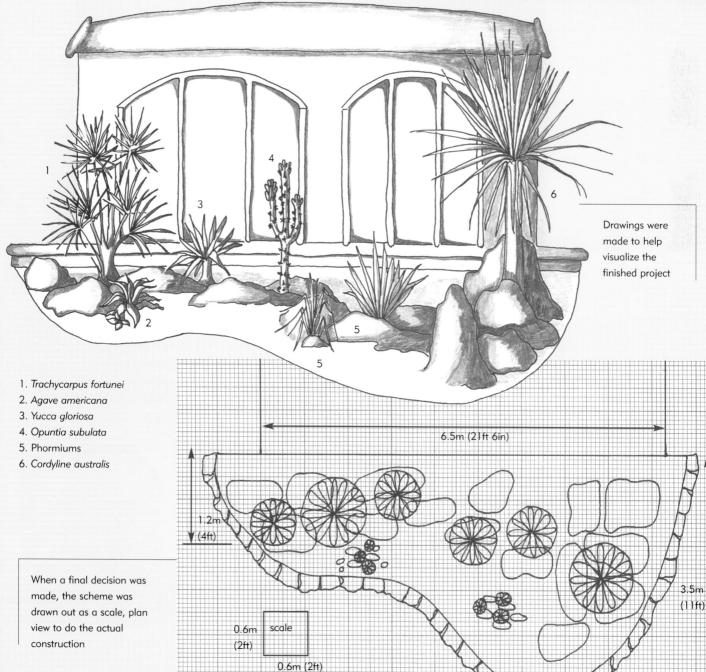

Drawings were made to help visualize the finished project

1. *Trachycarpus fortunei*
2. *Agave americana*
3. *Yucca gloriosa*
4. *Opuntia subulata*
5. *Phormiums*
6. *Cordyline australis*

6.5m (21ft 6in)

1.2m (4ft)

3.5m (11ft)

0.6m (2ft)   scale

0.6m (2ft)

When a final decision was made, the scheme was drawn out as a scale, plan view to do the actual construction

I also drew up a project sheet. It included:

Hard landscaping materials – permeable membrane, gravel, York stone; large rocks for features and smaller, flat paving pieces to create an edge between the lawn and the feature, to retain the gravel and to ensure that the grass could be kept mown. There were also assorted cobbles, individually chosen for colour and form to blend sympathetically with the York stone and gravel. (There were a few funny looks at the suppliers as I lined up various combinations of cobbles next to a polythene bag of gravel and a slab of rock for colour matching!)

Plants – the larger hardy plants chosen were *Yucca gloriosa*, *Yucca gloriosa* 'Variegata', *Trachycarpus fortunei*, *Cordyline australis*, *Phormium* 'Sundowner', and a smaller weeping *Phormium* 'Cream Delight'. The bed has been planted with their future growth and appearance in mind. There were 15 or so smaller plants to go amongst the cobbles chosen from colourful grasses, like *Uncinia rubra*, and *Carex oshimensis* 'Evergold', *Ophiopogon planiscapus* 'Nigrescens', and sedums and sempervivums.

Of course, alterations were made to the finished design because things don't always turn out the way you imagine. For example, the right hand curve projects further forwards than was originally planned because the angle had to be altered to ensure that the paved edge would be easy to mow along.

Rocks are obviously quarried in a variety of shapes, sizes and forms, which the design must take into account. In this case, we used less rounded pieces of stone than the original design suggested, and there was also an unexpected gap in the back of the large rock grouping on the right, which had to be filled. I chose *Phormium* 'Bronze Baby', which links well with the colours and shapes of the other planting, including the other phormiums and grasses.

The small groups of cobbles were also altered from two clusters, to a more regular distribution across the front of the whole bed, following the curve of the large rocks and the shape of the bed. Some were clumped in projecting outcrops to fill in the extra space resulting from the changed curve of the bed.

The message, then, is to plan well ahead, thoroughly and accurately. But don't forget to keep enough flexibility in your scheme to allow for unexpected problems, as well as for the occasional bonus of happy accidents.

Marking out the bed

Grass removed

Paving edge and large planting

Permeable membrane and gravel added

Above: adding rock

Right: completed – rocks, plants cobbles

Below: planting small plants through a membrane

1

Carefully clear away the gravel from the area where you want the plant to go

2

Cut a cross shape in the membrane with sharp scissors

3

Hold the membrane out of the way with stones or cobbles while you set the plant

4

Bed the plant in well, watering it in if the site is particularly dry, then put the membrane back around the plant and replace the gravel

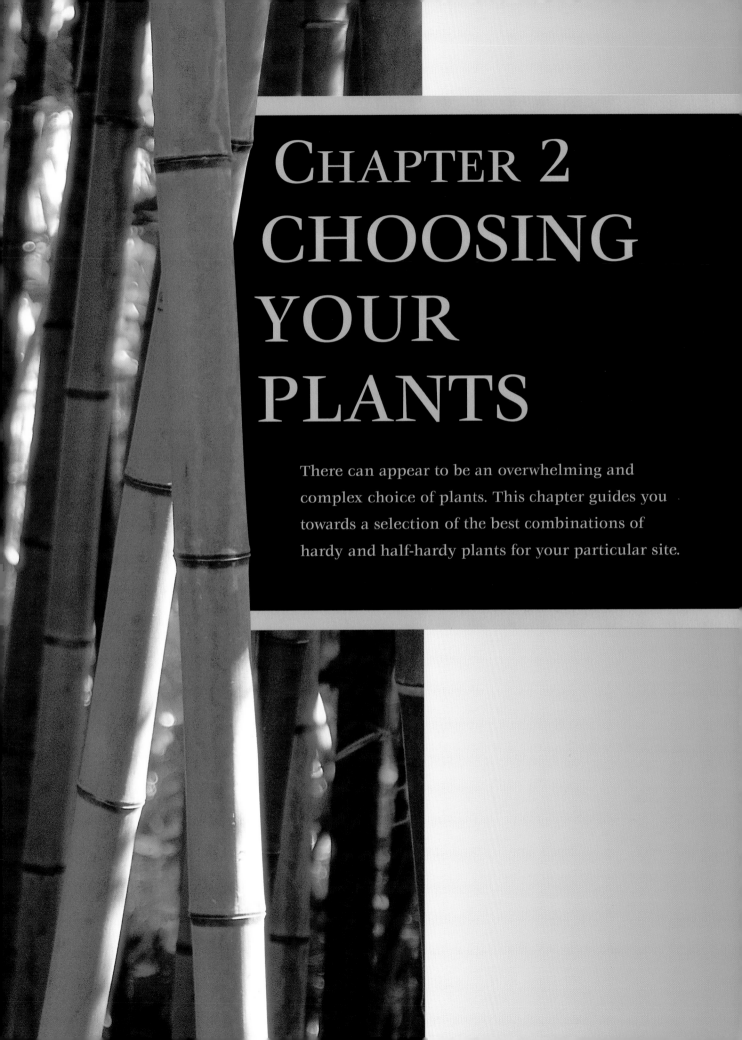

CHAPTER 2
CHOOSING YOUR PLANTS

There can appear to be an overwhelming and
complex choice of plants. This chapter guides you
towards a selection of the best combinations of
hardy and half-hardy plants for your particular site.

You can use an attractive mix of hardy and half-hardy subjects. In this case, l to r, foreground *Aloe aristata*, *Echeveria* 'Afterglow' and *Agave americana*, with *Echeveria* 'Perle von Nurnberg', grey-leaved *Cotyledon orbiculata* and trailing *Sedum lineare* 'Variegatum' in the background

Obviously, the choice of plants is the key for gardening with cacti and other succulents. The plants listed in this chapter can be regarded as the basic species and varieties. They will give your scheme a strength and unity of structure which is a must if you are not to have something which is both visually confusing and which introduces some of the higher maintenance choice of plant that you are trying to get away from.

Because each chapter which follows will refer to combinations of these plants they are described here to avoid unnecessary repetition – so it is worth bookmarking this section so you can flip backwards and forwards easily.

The plants are a mix of cacti and succulents with various degrees of hardiness, plus a selection of hardy architectural plants which associate very sympathetically because of their spiky angular forms and unusual colours. These architecturals are important in that they will give a permanent backbone structure to your garden and plant features, so that you don't have to endure a relatively barren and colourless winter when some of the less hardy plants have to be moved indoors.

Some plants, which have a more specialist function, will be described in detail in the specific chapter that they relate to. For example, Chapter 8, Combination Gardening, covers a wider range of plants for a mixed garden. This allows you to blend an otherwise uncompromising scheme into your existing garden, by gradually moving from starkly architectural forms to softer choices which will then drift into, for example, a conventional herbaceous border, or other feature. Because hardy, carpeting sedums are covered in detail in Chapter 6, Pools and Water Features, and as colour-themed choices for Carpet Bedding in Chapter 9, they will be referred to in this chapter, but for full descriptions, do read the relevant chapter, to avoid needless repetition.

The Plant Directory in Chapter 10 illustrates, in photographs and brief description, a large selection of plants for you to choose from as a foundation to your exotic gardening with cacti, succulents and architectural companion plants. They are selected for a number of features, including appearance, colour, vigour and ease of cultivation. Hopefully, you will browse in this section and use it as a springboard into further choices.

Also, on page 184, you will find a list of all the hardiest cacti and succulents and their synonyms, which is an invaluable guide if you want to immerse yourself in this area of gardening. This is an ongoing area of interest amongst enthusiasts, so some specialist sources for further information and updates can be found on pages 191–2, plus information on plant and garden associations, societies, books and websites.

'Duet' is another showy dwarf. This is a stiff spiky grower, ideal for small feature gardens and containers. It has slender, erect green leaves broadly banded with creamy white on both edges, and it reaches 0.6 x 0.6cm (2 x 2ft). 'Evening Glow' is a fabulous newer cultivar, which has graceful, arching red foliage with deeper red margins. 0.75 x 0.75m ($2^1/2$ x $2^1/2$ft). 'Jester' has very pretty pale pink leaves, striped with green.

'Rainbow Sunrise', (syn. 'Maori Sunrise'). This is a very colourful, small upright cultivar with fine, slender leaves, light red to orange shades edged with bronze. Reaches 1 x 1m (3 x 3ft). Gorgeous!

'Rainbow Maiden', (syn. 'Maori Maiden'), is very showy, with delicate weeping leaves in rich, rosy salmon pink to coral red, banded with bronze margins. It makes a wonderful container plant. Reaches 0.75 x 0.75m ($2^1/2$ x $2^1/2$ft).

SMALLER BAMBOOS

Pleioblastus chino f. *elegantissimus*, reaches a height of 0.5–1m (20in–3ft) and withstands temperatures down to -18°C (0°F). It is an ideal choice for a container or it makes an attractive and unusual edging. It is, in fact, an unusual bamboo, whose mass of variegated slender green leaves with white stripes, and its bushy, though elegant waving habit gives it a lovely frothy appearance. It is tolerant, growing happily anywhere in sun or shade.

× *Hibanobambusa tranquillans* f. *kimmei* is ideal for ground cover and wonderful for planting in groups. It bears dark green leaves with yellow stripes on short slender stems, and reaches a height of 1–2m (3–$6^1/2$ft) and it likes sun and half shade.

× *Hibanobambusa tranquillans* 'Shiroshima' has green canes and strikingly variegated, equally striped green and yellow leaves,

which are relatively large at 23cm (9in) long x 4cm ($1^1/2$in) wide, and tinted pink when young. It grows to about 1.8m (6ft).

Pleioblastus pygmaeus var. *distichus* is a very compact bamboo with fine green leaves on green upright stems. It is good for ground cover or for group planting, and it likes a position in full sun. It grows to 0.5–1m (20in–3ft), and stands down to -20°C (-4°F).

Bamboos, with their slender canes and delicate leaves, make attractive specimen plants for containers. However, they will need plenty of water

Pleioblastus variegatus (syn. *Arundinaria fortunei*) is one of the best of the white-striped variegated bamboos. This is a low-growing species, with zigzag pale green canes, reaching 0.75–1.2m (2¹/₂–4ft) high, bearing dark green leaves with white stripes which are 5–20cm (2–8in) long and 1–2.5cm (¹/₂–1in) wide. Its tufted habit makes it a lovely subject for the rock garden, and for containers.

Pleioblastus viridistriatus carries green and yellow variegated leaves on thin upright canes. It has a compact spreading habit which means that it is good for mixed planting, however it does need shade. It grows to 1–1.5m (3–5ft), and will survive down to -23°C (-9°F).

Pleioblastus viridistriatus 'Auricoma' (syn. *Arundinaria auricoma*) is one of the best of the variegated bamboos, with attractive dark green leaves striped with rich yellow, often carrying more yellow than green on variable sized leaves from 7.5–20cm (3–8in) long and 1–4cm (¹/₂–1¹/₂in) wide. It has thin, erect, purplish-green canes, 1–2m (3–6¹/₂ft) high and it has a compact spreading habit. It is ideal for mixed planting and for use as a specimen plant. Old canes can be cut down in autumn to encourage brightly coloured new foliage. It does, however, need shade. It grows to about 0.75–1m (2¹/₂–3ft) and it is very hardy as it withstands -23°C (-9°F).

Pseudosasa japonica (*Arundinaria japonica*) has olive green canes and masses of glossy, dark green evergreen leaves with grey undersides. It grows to 3–4.5m (9–15ft) high and occasionally a metre higher and it forms dense, arching thickets, which makes it good for use as screening, but it is tolerant and adaptable so it is also good for containers.

Sasa tessellata. This bamboo has the largest leaves, carried on green arching stems growing 1–2m (3–6¹/₂ft) tall. It is hardy down to -18°C (0°F).

Sasa palmata has wide green leaves on curving stems, which grow with attractive layers of leaves. A fast-growing species, which likes sun or shade, and reaches 1.5–2m (5–6¹/₂ft) high, and is frost hardy to -18°C (0°F).

Sasaella masamuneana f. *albostriata*. This bushy, compact species has dark green leaves with yellow-white stripes on upright zigzag stems. It enjoys sun or shade. It reaches 1–2m (3–6¹/₂ft) high, and tolerates down to -18°C (0°F).

CACTI

Smaller hardy opuntias like:

Opuntia compressa, syn. *O. humifusa*. Prostrate spreading padded plants with large yellow flowers, hardy in a well-drained rockery.

Opuntia polyacantha. These are bushy, prostrate plants with spiny pads and bearing yellow flowers. Hardy on well drained rockery.

The golden and green variegated leaves of *Pleioblastus viridistriatus* make a vivid display in a shady position

An old wok makes an unusual container for hardy *Sedum acre* 'Yellow Queen', *Crassula sarcocaulis*, Sedum spathulifolium 'Cape Blanco', *S. album* f. *murale* 'Coral Carpet' along with saxifraga and sempervivums

OTHER SUCCULENTS

There is a marvellous range of hardy, colourful, evergreen carpeting succulents, which are described at length in Chapter 8, Pools and Water Features, and Chapter 10, Carpet Bedding, including the following:

Lewisias

Mesembryanthemum 'Basutoland' *R

Saxifragas *R
Saxifraga aizoon
Saxifraga × *correvonensis*
Saxifraga cuneifolia variegata
Saxifraga 'Southside Seedling'

Sedums *R
Sedum acre 'Yellow Queen'
Sedum album var. *micranthum* subvar. *chloroticum*
Sedum album f. *murale* 'Coral Carpet'
Sedum × *amecamecanum*
Sedum cauticola Lidakense'
Sedum ellacombianum

Sedum ewersii 'Nanum'
Sedum hispanicum

Sedum lydium
Sedum middendorffianum
Sedum pachyclados
Sedum pluricaule
Sedum spathulifolium 'Cape Blanco'
Sedum spathulifolium var. *purpureum*
Sedum spurium var. *variegatum*
Sedum spurium

Sempervivums
(house leeks) *R

Easy-going, colourful sempervivum cultivars are hardy 'must-haves'

Section 2: Hardy in milder areas of the UK

THIS SECTION INCLUDES PLANTS THAT WILL SURVIVE IN MILDER AREAS OF BRITAIN.

These plants will survive in the south of Britain, in city microclimates, and in the drier and lower-lying regions; however, in wet and or hilly areas, the far north of England and in Scotland, they will need winter protection (fleece, bubble wrap or straw) or to be treated as half-hardy subjects.

TALL ACCENT PLANTS

PALMS
Less hardy than the palms in Section 1, but surviving happily in the southwest of England, and in parts of the east, is *Phoenix canariensis*, the Canary Island date palm. This has an attractive feathery form, with stiff, dark green arching leaves. It will thrive in sun or shade and will stand a lot of frost. Plants over 1.5m (5ft) tall are hardier.

CORDYLINES
These are also known as the Cornish or Torquay palms, and they are very dramatic, architectural 'surrogate' palms, although they are actually succulents as they belong to the Agavaceae family. They are slow-growing evergreens which have sword-like leaves surrounding a woody stem; as this grows the leaves die off and they can then be stripped back, with a sharp downwards tug, to reveal an attractive trunk. These are hardy in almost all circumstances; at worst they are cut down in a severe winter, but they will resprout vigorously in the spring, producing a multi-headed plant which can be divided

when the stems become woody. Alternatively, in less favourable areas, they can be treated as a dramatic potted subject for half-hardy display in the warmer months, and moved into a conservatory for the winter.

Cordyline australis, is a vigorous green-leaved version of this hardy 'palm', which produces

Cordyline australis a 'surrogate' palm which is hardy in much of Britain, in bud

heads of white flowers in the summer. It grows readily from seed. It reaches 15m (50ft) eventually, with 30cm–1m (1–3ft) long leaves and summer panicles of small white flowers.

Cordyline indivisa, is very similar in appearance to *australis*, with a darker mid-stripe to the leaves. It is smaller, growing to 3m (9ft) or so with a spread of 2m (6$\frac{1}{2}$ft) with 0.6m–2m (2–6$\frac{1}{2}$ft) long leaves and clusters of small white flowers.

The showier hybrids are slightly less vigorous and make small trees with time. For variegation, look at:

Cordyline 'Albertii', a really dramatic, variegated cordyline with green and white striped leaves.

'Sundance' has attractive olive green leaves with a red mid-stripe and narrower red lines.

For unusual colour choices, which make excellent contrast with summer bedding, try:

'Coffee Cream', with olive brown leaves with a yellowish mid-stripe.

'Purple Tower', deep red-brown.

'Red Star', dramatic bronze-red.

OTHER CHOICES

Another curiosity is the tree fern *Dicksonia antarctica*, a primitive plant from Australia. It is a tree-like fern that resembles a palm with a stout trunk covered with brown fibres, which are actually aerial roots. In the summer the plant is crowned with arching, much divided palm-like fronds, a metre or more long. In the winter these will die back, and the heart of the plant should be protected with hay or sacking pushed down into the centre. Once it starts growing again the fronds grow at a ferocious rate, but the trunk itself grows at a rate of only around 2.5cm (1in) per year.

MEDIUM RANGE PLANTS

SUCCULENTS

Agaves have already been described in the 'Hardy' section (see page 26). The following species are almost hardy in Britain, and will certainly survive in milder or drier areas of the country, especially in a well-drained position, e.g. in a rockery. We have several long-lived specimens in various positions in the gardens at our nursery in south Lincolnshire. Furthermore, any slight damage is incidental as the plant grows by replacing its older leaves, so damage will grow out in time. However, because these are freely offsetting plants, you can always hedge your bets, and keep some spares tucked away in the warm as a back-up.

In less favourable areas, because it is wet, rather than cold conditions, to which they succumb in the winter months, the plants can be left in place in the garden under overhead shelter, e.g. if you have an overhanging porch, for example – or by rigging temporary protection with a cold frame or bubble polythene. Otherwise, they will spend the winter happily in unheated sheds, greenhouses and outhouses if kept totally dry.

Agave americana is the best known of the agaves. It is also known as the century plant, because it only flowers when huge (though it does not take 100 years!). These are definitely the triffids of the agave family, as, with time, the plants can reach up to 2m (6$\frac{1}{2}$ft) in height with a 2–3m (6$\frac{1}{2}$–9ft) spread. It has dark blue-green leaves, the backs of which are imprinted very attractively with the ghostly jagged pattern of the adjacent leaves, which happens as the leaves are growing, tightly furled together in the bud.

Agave filifera, or thread agave, is another attractive and borderline hardy species, which has long, narrow and tapering glossy green leaves with white margins, which split away, to form an edging of long white fibres. *Agave stricta* is very unusual and well worth looking for. It grows up to 1m (3ft) across and forms large, spherical heads of long, thin, tapering leaves like a giant bobble on a hat.

Look out, too, for *Aloe aristata*, which is a narrow-leaved rosette, with a very tall flower stalk and orange red flowers and is hardy in a well-drained rockery.

Echinocereus viridiflorus in flower nestled in a rockery

SMALLER PLANTS

CACTI
Cacti stand a very good chance of survival if they can have a sunny well-drained position.

Chamaecereus* (syn. lobivia or chamaelobivia, or peanut cacti) have been widely hybridized. They are small, clustering cacti which flower freely, and are renowned for being remarkably tough. The species is *Chamaecereus silvestrii*, which carries bright scarlet flowers. Some of the interesting hybrids include gold-, lilac- and white-flowered plants, which are all worth a try. Look out for 'Devon Dawn', with yellow flowers; 'Sunset', with abundant flowers in shades of orange and red; and 'Ragged Robin', with purple-red flowers with 'ragged' petals. 'Harry Cammack' has pretty salmon flowers, while 'Greenpeace' has pale yellow flowers with a green mid-stripe.

Echinocereus* is a genus of over 70 species of showy plants often with attractive spines and colourful flowers up to 12cm (5in) across. Plants can be globular, columnar or trailing. *Echinocereus chloranthus* makes small, fine-spined, clusters of stems to 25cm (10in) tall, bearing numerous small, greenish flowers. *Echinocereus engelmannii*, has freely branching stems up to 20cm (8in) high, which are pale green and thickly covered with long stiff spines of various colours. It has large purplish-red flowers with toothed petals.

Echinocereus fendleri forms small dark-bodied clumps of stems, each about 12–15cm (5–6in) high and 5–7.5cm (2–3in) wide, sparsely spined, with deep pink flowers.
Echinocereus pectinatus is an erect cylindrical species covered in short white or pink spines often changing colour in zones up the plant. It has pink flowers with a white centre.
Echinocereus pentalophus has long, thick, pale green sprawling stems. Its flowers are up to 12cm (5in) long, lilac or pink with a white throat.
Echinocereus reichenbachii has cylindrical stems up to 20cm (8in) high covered in fine yellow spines. It bears large pink flowers.
Echinocereus triglochidiatus has sparse, but long, white and black spines and carries long-lasting deep red flowers.
Echinocereus viridiflorus is an offsetting

species producing unusual yellowish-green flowers.

Echinopsis* are easily grown plants often clustering with age. Most species have spectacular and very large tubular flowers. In some species the flowers open at night and are perfumed.

Echinopsis eyriesii is a reliable bloomer, with huge white flowers which are up to 25cm (10in) long. Magnificent!

Echinopsis leucantha has large pure white flowers.

Echinopsis oxygona has very large bright pink flowers.

Echinopsis rhodotricha has very large pure white flowers.

Echinopsis silvestrii. This plant readily produces incredible, 20cm (8in) long, pure white flowers. It has to be seen to be believed!

Echinopsis tubiflora also produces huge white flowers.

Lobivia* is a genus of small, compact plants with large flowers in dazzling reds, yellows, pinks and white.

Lobivia aurea. White-spined plants with lemon yellow flowers with deep yellow centres.

Lobivia chrysantha bears 6cm (2¹/₂in) long, yellow flowers with a red throat.

Lobivia haematantha subsp. *densispina* has white, close-cropped spines and lemon yellow flowers with a white throat.

Lobivia marsoneri are beautiful, blue-grey plants with black spines. The flowers are yellow, with a red throat.

Lobivia schreiteri is a dark green clustering plant with showy flowers, which are orange to dark red with black throats.

Notocactus* is a deservedly popular genus of globular or short columnar plants with a range of spination. Their showy flowers appear in a wide variety of colours and are reliably produced.

Notocactus buiningii is attractive even when not in flower because of its light, grass green colour, symmetrical ribs and spination. It bears very large, yellow flowers.

Notocactus concinnus has very showy, funnel-shaped flowers with reddish outer petals and satiny, canary yellow inner ones.

Notocactus herteri is noteworthy for its fine, glossy, deep purplish-red flowers in a genus with mainly yellow blooms.

Notocactus mammulosus has large canary yellow flowers.

Notocactus roseoluteus. These are coppery-green plants with a crown covered in white wool, and which carry particularly large, bell-shaped, glossy flowers in shades of salmon and yellow.

Notocactus rutilans is an unusual and choice species, with large carmine flowers, shading to yellow and white in the throat.

Notocactus schlosseri has glossy lemon yellow flowers with light green mid-stripe.

Notocactus schumannianus is a columnar species, growing up to 0.9m (35in) tall. It has many ribs with fine yellow spines and large, pure yellow flowers.

Lobivia hertrichiana will grow and flower outside in a sheltered, free-draining spot

Section 3: Half-hardy plants

This section includes plants that need protection or to be moved indoors during winter.

Adding half-hardy species and varieties gives a dramatically increased range of plants to extend your garden projects. They can stay out once the danger of frost has passed, from late spring to mid-autumn. All of the cacti and other succulents will appreciate an airing and the succulents will colour up especially well in daylight. You will also find that the plants become stronger and more resilient because they have had to cope with wind and weather.

TALL ACCENT PLANTS

CACTI
There is a huge variety of tall, columnar half-hardy cacti, which will grow in time into a spiny forest of spiky columns.

Carnegiea gigantea, the large-branching and famous cowboy cactus, but it takes years to grow to its full size.

Cephalocereus chrysacanthus, tall-growing, branching, slender columns with yellowish spines and large, pinkish-red flowers.
Cephalocereus senilis, or the old man cactus, has masses of tangled, long white hair. Large prize specimens have been known to be shampooed and brushed in readiness for making an appearance on show benches. Slow growing.

Cereus aethiops is a slender species reaching about 1.5–1.8m (5–6ft). The flowers, which are white, sometimes flushed pink, are produced at an earlier stage than most cereus.
Cereus alacriportanus has tall, bluish-green cylindrical stems up to 2m (6½ft) tall. Old specimens bear huge, 23cm (9in) long, very pale yellowish-pink flowers.
Cereus chalybaeus, forms attractive bluish columns, 5cm (2in) or more thick, bearing black spines on well-defined ribs.
Cereus forbesii forms blue-grey columns growing several metres high in the wild! Vigorous growers 'in captivity'.
Cereus hankeanus is a tall-growing, cylindrical plant, which will grow rapidly to give height to a collection. They will eventually grow to a few metres high. They have large, white 12cm (5in) long flowers.
Cereus jamacaru grows into bluish-green ribbed columns up to a metre tall eventually with very large white flowers.
Cereus peruvianus has tall-growing blue-green columns with six to eight ribs. Large white flowers are carried on old specimens.
Cereus validus has bluish-green ribbed columns up to 2m (6½ft) high and large white to reddish flowers. Quick growing.

Cleistocactus candelilla has columnar stems, up to 1m (3ft) high, bearing tubular purple flowers with a white border.
Cleistocactus morawetzianus has a shrubby or tree-like body with grey-green stems, pale spines and long white flowers with a greenish or faintly pink sheen.
Cleistocactus straussii has beautiful soft white spines. This is a columnar species, bearing strange, almost rudimentary, long scarlet flowers.

Haageocereus multangularis is a vigorous, columnar plant, offsetting from the base, and covered in fine, rusty yellow spines. It eventually grows to 1m (3ft) high and bears nocturnal lilac and red flowers.

Haageocereus churinensis has tall columns with orange-yellow spines, clustering in time. Large strongly perfumed white flowers are carried on older plants.

Haageocereus limensis forms quick-growing tall columns with brown and grey spines and carrying large tubular flowers.

Haageocereus multangularis var. *pseudomelanostele* has tall clustering stems covered in thin yellow spines and large greenish-white flowers.

Haageocereus winterianus grows with tall branching stems, with dark golden yellow spines. The plant eventually reaches up to a few metres tall and eventually produces large white flowers.

Haageocereus johnsonii is tall growing, with a branching trunk covered in fine, soft golden yellow spines and carrying huge, faintly perfumed, delicate pink flowers.

Haagoecereus versicolor has dark green columnar stems to 1m (3ft) tall with yellowish-brown spines and large white flowers.

Opuntia cylindrica, tall-growing cylindrical plants with large yellow flowers.

Opuntia jamaicensis has lightly spined oval pads. It readily produces its sulphur yellow 4cm (1^1/$_2$in) diameter flowers.

Opuntia subulata, similar to *O. cylindrica*. Rapidly growing clustering columns. This plant has the advantage that you can lop off the top section, let the cut end callous over in a dry, shady position for two weeks or so, then pot in it in slightly damp, gritty compost, when it will reroot. The cut section on the original plant will sprout several new heads, so that you can have a series of candelabra-like cacti.

Oreocereus (syn. borzicactus)
Oreocereus celsianus, tall growing and covered in wispy white hair.

Oreocereus celsianus var. *hendriksenianus* has fast-growing, tall hairy columns with few but stout spines and red tubular flowers.

Oreocereus celsianus var. *fossulatus* grows up to 2m (6^1/$_2$ft) tall, has long wispy white hairs and violet-red flowers.

Oreocereus celsianus var. *trollii* is tall growing with dense fine white hairs.

Trichocereus (syn. echinopsis)
Trichocereus candicans is a branching, tall-growing cowboy-type cactus, bearing large, 20cm (8in) long, strongly perfumed white flowers.

Trichocereus macrogona has tall, stout bluish-green, branching stems and huge white flowers.

Half-hardy *Opuntia subulata* makes an exotic summer companion to a hardy, all year round planting of yuccas and phormiums

Trichocereus spachiana has tall, dark green columns, freely branching, with impressive night-flowering blooms to 20cm (8in) long by 15cm (6in) wide, which have white inner petals and greenish-tinged outer petals.
Trichocereus valida. These are stout, erect columnar, fast-growing plants with large white flowers.
Trichocereus courantii, grows into thick columns with yellowish spines. Quick-growing with very large rose-scented flowers.

OTHER SUCCULENTS
Taller-growing succulents include:

Aloe arborescens which has a stout, tall-growing stem up to 2m (6^1/$_2$ft), with dark green fleshy rosettes of strongly toothed tapering leaves. It bears tubular red flowers on a long stem.
Aloe gariepensis has branching stems to 1m (3ft) high, with dark green leaves with white spots and horny edges. It has a tall inflorescence with yellow flowers.

Crassula arborescens is a shrub which can grow up to 4m (12ft) tall with gorgeous blue-grey leaves with red edges.

Parallel evolution in Africa has resulted in the cactus-like architectural euphorbias, which are also branching candelabra-like plants, and will give summer height to your bedding. Look for:
Euphorbia candelabrum var. *erythraea*, which has dark green stems with a lighter green central band. This forms branches like a candelabrum with small leaves.
Euphorbia cooperi is another wonderful candelabrum with stout, branching columns, four or five angled, with flat sides between. It eventually becomes very tall.
Euphorbia enopla has branching, thorny six to seven angled stems, growing up to 1m (3ft) high. It has small, yellow flowers.

MEDIUM RANGE PLANTS

CACTI
Again there is a good selection of columnar cacti for your vertical emphasis and accent.

Cleistocactus brookei has tall, cylindrical stems, growing up to 0.5m (20in) high, with yellowish spines, and peculiar s-shaped red flowers, which are 5cm (2in) long.
Cleistocactus villamontesii forms branching columns up to 4m (16in) high with numerous tubular purple and white flowers.

Opuntia robusta has succulent blue-green pads with a beautiful grey bloom and few spines. It has yellow flowers.

Trichocereus schickendantzii has tall columns, branching from the base, up to 25cm (10in) high. It carries huge white flowers with green outer petals.

OTHER SUCCULENTS
There is also a good selection of species of middle-height succulents.

Aeoniums are attractive branching plants.
Aeonium arboreum 'Atropurpureum' has branching stems with very attractive deep maroon rosettes.
Aeonium arboreum has tall stems, which can be induced to branch into an attractive candelabrum by cutting off and rerooting the top, as described under *Opuntia subulata* (see page 41). It bears bright green rosettes and grows up to 1m (3ft) high. It bears tall golden yellow flowers. *Aeonium arboreum* 'Variegatum' is its lovely variegated form.

An easy-care gravel bed planted with *Agave americana* and *A. americana* 'Variegata' surrounding the almost black rosettes of *Aeonium arboreum* 'Zwartkop'

it through the winter in Lincolnshire). An unheated outhouse is perfectly suitable for winter storage if the plants are kept dry although, again, it is a crime to hide their light under a bushel as they are such handsome plants for interior display.

Agave americana 'Variegata' is a showier relative of *A. americana*, with broad yellow edges to the leaves. It has a height and spread of 2m ($6^1/_2$ft) and offsets freely, like its plainer relative. *A. americana* 'Mediopicta' is another variegated form with a cream to yellow central stripe and green edges to its leaves; it also grows to 2 x 2m ($6^1/_2$ x $6^1/_2$ft).

Look out, too, for smaller, slower-growing forms, like *Agave ferdinandi-regis*, with attractive rosettes of triangular leaves edged with white and the glorious *A. victoriae-reginae*, the 'royal agave', with spineless dark rosettes of deep glossy green leaves, white striped and edged, with black, needle-like spikes on the tips.

Aeonium domesticum is a small shrub with branching stems and oval, slightly hairy, green and cream leaves.

Aeonium haworthia 'Variegatum' is a colourful succulent which has fleshy leaves in peach, cream and green.

Aeonium arboreum 'Zwartkop' is a wonderful companion planting to *A. arboreum*, with very impressive, glossy purple rosettes on long stems which become black when planted outside.

AGAVES

Some of the most coveted agaves are the variegated forms. The variegated forms are tender, and definitely need winter protection, (though *Agave americana* 'Variegata' has made

ALOES

These are also good strong rosette-forming architectural succulents, which look especially good in pots and grouped in troughs, window boxes and other containers in the summer months.

Aloe haworthioides has very attractive rosettes, with light green pointed leaves with white marks. Its flowers are orange, on a long stalk.

Aloe ferox has fiercely spined succulent grey leaves.

Aloe melanacantha has open rosettes of tapering leaves with white horny teeth and tall yellow to red flowers.

Aloe striata forms stemless rosettes, which have leaves 0.4–0.5m (16–20in) long with white marginal teeth and produces coral red flowers.

Aloe vera has long tapering leaves, usually spotted white. It will form dense groups and the plants bear yellow flowers.

Aloe variegata, or the 'partridge-breasted' aloe, has thick green, triangular leaves attractively variegated with white and it carries red flowers on a long stem.

Alworthia 'Black Gem' is an interesting and coveted hybrid of aloe and haworthia which has dramatic black-green leaves when grown in full sun.

CRASSULAS

Crassula ovata (syn. *C. argentea* or *C. portulacea*) or the money plant. Excellent as a miniature tree, reaching up to 1m (3ft) high with time. It carries small white flowers in winter.

Crassula ovata (syn. *C. argentea* or *C. portulacea*) 'Blue Bird'. Another form of the money plant with grey-green leaves. This is also excellent as a miniature tree.

Crassula ovata (syn. *C. argentea* or *C. portulacea*) 'Hummel's Sunset' is a colourful form of the money plant, which is attractively variegated yellow and red, and especially showy when grown in strong light.

Crassula obliqua 'Variegata' is a thinner-leaved money plant with yellowish, cream and pale green leaves.

Crassula ovata 'Hummel's Sunset' is particularly colourful when it can enjoy natural light outdoors in the summer months

EUPHORBIAS

Euphorbia fimbriata has pale green and much- branched stems reminiscent of miniature 'cowboy cacti' and carries yellow flowers.

Euphorbia fasciculata has green columns with rudimentary leaves. It carries small yellow flowers on a long stalk.

Euphorbia trigona has attractive three or four angled stems, red leaves, often with white or red mottling. It forms a shrub eventually.

SMALLER PLANTS

Cotyledon orbiculata is an attractive miniature tree-like plant with a delicate grey bloom.

CRASSULA

Mat-forming *Crassula pellucida* subsp. *marginalis* becomes almost maroon in strong light and carries white flowers; *C. socialis* and *C. volkensii* are good choices for trailing over the edges of half-hardy containers.

Crassula sarmentosa 'Variegata' has long, trailing stems up to 1m (3ft) long, and curling at the tips. The leaves are variegated white and green, sometimes with some red.

ECHEVERIA

These half-hardy plants form lovely, pastel-coloured or brightly coloured rosettes that make large plants in time. They come in a range of colours from palest lilac, grey and turquoise to scarlet and deep purple and every shade of green. They are good for unusual summer bedding displays and they are the favoured choice for carpet bedding. Try them in a container surrounding a taller, more architectural plant like a cordyline, or an agave or aeonium. Also ideal for pots, patios, conservatories and as tolerant house plants. Look out for:

Echeveria affinis, which has impressive dark olive green rosettes, almost black in full sun.
Echeveria albicans has powdery grey-blue leaves, forming an attractive rosette, and orange flowers.
Echeveria 'Black Prince', like all the dark echeveria, is a highly prized 'catch'. It has red-maroon to almost black leaves.
Echeveria 'Blue Curls' forms rosettes of wavy blue-green leaves.
Echeveria 'Easter Bonnet' has lovely blue-grey leaves with crinkled edges.
Echeveria 'Mexican Firecracker' has colourful rosettes of 'felt'-covered leaves, which are strikingly brown-red below and green above. It has orange flowers.
Echeveria 'Painted Frills' has rosettes of wavy red, brown and olive green leaves and bears yellow flowers.
Echeveria peacockii has rosettes of long tapering blue-white leaves and produces intense red flowers.
Echeveria 'Perle von Nurnberg' is an amazing and very pretty lilac-leafed hybrid with geranium pink flowers.
See also graptopetalum, which is a related genus, and graptoveria which are hybrids of echeveria and graptopetalum.

KALANCHOE
The trailing kalanchoes like *K. manginii**, *K.* 'Mirabella'* and *K.* 'Wendy'* flower prolifically and look wonderful in hanging baskets and window boxes.

SEDUM
Trailing half-hardy species include:
Sedum morganianum, or donkey's tail, which is a beautiful grey succulent trailing plant.
Sedum morganianum × *Echeveria derenbergii* is a choice hybrid of donkey's tail. This is a trailing plant with cascades of succulent grey leaves, stouter than *S. morganianum*, and

terminating in clumps of red flowers.
Sedum nussbaumerianum will stand slight frost. It has orange-gold stems with club-shaped leaves a few cm (1in or so) long. *S. adolphii* is also very similar and will withstand slight frost.
Sedum × *rubrotinctum*, often found under the name of *S. guatemalense*, is a very colourful trailing plant with glossy red and green club-shaped leaves. There is also a pink-leaved trailing variety. Both of these are almost hardy and are worth risking in a mild winter. (Keep some plants inside too though, as a security measure.)

Senecio rowleyanus, the string of beads, makes trailing cascades of pea green spheres, like a living bead curtain.

OTHER CHOICES

See Chapter 9, Combination Gardening, for a wide range of good associated plants including armeria* (thrift), eryngiums (sea hollies), heucheras including 'Palace Purple', *Ophiopogon planiscapus* 'Nigrescens' – a long name for a wonderful black grass-like subject, plus ornamental grasses (R) like *Carex secta* var. *tenuiculmis* or *Phalaris arundinacea* var. *picta*. There are also lots of good exotic, 'hot-looking' flowering subjects like kniphofia mixed hybrids* (red hot pokers), strelitzia* (bird of paradise), cannas* and many more.

Echeverias make a colourful planting in this large, wire basket. The mingled pastel shades of large-leaved *E. glauca* and smaller *E. secunda* and *E.* 'Perle von Nurnberg'

CHAPTER 3
GRAVEL AND
SCREE BEDS

Gravel and scree beds are a dramatic
and eye-catching way to transform
all or part of your garden.

APPLICATIONS

In a gravel bed, the whole surface of a bed, border or other feature is covered with a mulch comprised of an assortment of materials which can range from a layer of fine gravel, like pea shingle, to coloured chippings, or bark. For the more adventurous there are various other materials to choose from ranging from shells, to industrial waste glass which has been transformed into a smooth covering material in the form of fine glass pebbles with no sharp edges. The Chelsea Flower Show (held annually in London) has featured all sorts of adventurous materials, including a selection of brass washers which offers an interesting, non-rusting but expensive, surfacing material.

Scree gardens differ in that the gravel surface is used in combination with carefully selected pieces of larger material. This larger material consists of either rounded or jagged rock forms, in diminishing sizes. For example, from large water-smoothed boulders, through cobbles to small rounded pebbles, or larger pieces of rock diminishing gradually in size until there is a rough scree of broken rock pieces blending into the gravel. The conceit here is that there is a reference to the natural scree features, which form at the bottom of steep cliff faces, where the rocks lie in a jumble. In scree gardening the scree area can link a gravel bed to a rockery, or the larger rocks and stones can act as extra features, chosen and 'planted' almost in the same way that the living specimens are, and used to bind the scheme together as a whole.

Both gravel and scree gardens are very flexible because they have so many applications. They can be used for a single border, an island bed, a front garden, or the awkward weedy strip along the edge of a drive.

The shapes and colours of *Agave americana*, *A. americana* 'Variegata', pale *Cotyledon orbiculata*, *Echeveria dereceana*, *E.* 'Afterglow' and *Sedum lineare* 'Variegatum' blend harmoniously together against the warm tones of the gravel

The smaller gardens of newer houses are particularly suitable for these schemes because they have such a high visual impact and make a more dramatic statement than anything else you may consider. Trying to fit a traditional garden into the space can be really frustrating. Gravel and scree gardens make much more sense in a smaller space than trying to fit in a tiny lawn and surrounding it with a high-maintenance border, with the nightmare task of keeping the grass regularly mown, weed free and neatly edged.

Phormium 'Rainbow Maiden' (syn. 'Maori Maiden') makes a splash of colour all year round

Gravel and scree beds also offer a flexible solution to access to the house and garage. Paths and drives can look stark and take up almost all of a front garden. With a gravel bed, you can make judicious use of paving slabs amongst the gravel to construct an attractive and integrated path to the house. Gravel makes a good surface for a drive but you need a good layer of compacted hard core underneath for it to take the weight of vehicles. With careful planning, you can have attractive groups of larger plants around the periphery of the car parking and manoeuvring areas. In the centre of a drive, where the middle of the car but not the wheels, will pass over them, you can use plantings of tough, spreading and low-growing hardy succulents, like jovibarbas, orostachys, sedums, saxifrages and sempervivums. Look at Chapters 6 and 9 for information on these plant selections. Because cars can actually drive in and park over this planting, you do not waste any precious planting space, which means that the whole area looks co-ordinated and attractive when the car isn't there.

These planting schemes are also the busy person's answer to gardening because, with the use of a permeable membrane under the

This sheltered hardy cactus and succulent garden, with *Agave parrasana*, *Opuntia basilaris* and a small *Aloe brevifolia* to the right, shows an interesting use of gravel and larger, rounded cobbles

gravel, they are extremely low maintenance. Just think of the advantages. At its most radical, the lawns could go altogether. This could mean the end of the weekend tyranny of the lawn mower, with all the concomitant chores of strimming and edging, feeding and moss-killing. It also means that there will be far less weeding of beds and borders and far more time to enjoy the garden.

SITING

As already discussed, careful planning is essential. In this case, these beds have to be sited in a defined area, with a definite demarcation between the gravel and the next material, be it grass, garden soil or hard landscaping. You don't want gravel or other top dressing straying into lawns, or grass growing into the gravel. If your lawn has too big a hold on your affections and has therefore been reprieved, add a strip of paving or other edging to run between the edge of the gravel bed and the edge of the lawn. If its profile is lower than the lawn, you can mow straight over the edges, which maintains a tidy boundary between your different garden areas.

As already discussed, if you want to grow the widest range of plants, the bed should be south- or southwest-facing and a wall at the back of the site will increase the range of plants you can use, because it will give shelter and act as a 'storage heater'. Also consider windproofing the bed with larger plants, or fencing or trellis.

CONSTRUCTION

For low maintenance, you must use a permeable membrane, which lets moisture through to the roots but suppresses weeds. I really cannot stress this point too strongly, because it is easy to use, relatively cheap and will save literally hours and hours of work in the long run. Contrary to popular belief, gravel doesn't kill weeds, so don't believe any one who tells you that gravel is a perfect, weed-suppressing mulch. People are advised to plant seeds and cuttings in a sharp mixture of gritty compost – in effect in a gravel bed! Unlined gravel over soil is a perfect seedbed for every plant and weed within bird, wind or pet transmission.

Black polythene is a short term solution, but it will eventually become brittle and crack in daylight, especially where the gravel has moved and exposed it to daylight and it will also collect standing water. However, permeable membrane is ultra-violet stabilized so that it will not become brittle and perish. It is water permeable so that puddles do not form on the surface, and it has a dense black finish, which suppresses the growth of weeds and prevents the roots of your cultivated plants from surfacing. It is also air permeable, so that the soil does not become sour or acidified. The membrane comes on a roll; you can choose from a variety of widths from 0.5m (20in) to 5m (16ft) wide, although a metre width is probably the easiest to manage. It is usually printed with 'tramlines',

Half-hardy *Opuntia subulata* with *Yucca elephantipes* (possibly hardy) in the background make a stark architectural planting in this gravel bed

If you have a large area to cover, cut down the undergrowth and roll out the membrane to smother the weeds. Anchor each strip with bricks or stones until you put the gravel on

so that it is easy to line up one sheet with another, and to plant in straight lines, if necessary.

Clear the site, removing as many weeds as possible. You can consider a scorched earth policy with herbicides such as Tumbleweed or Roundup, which will take about three weeks to kill weeds in all but will give you a clean site. If you are replacing a lawn, skim off the turf for use elsewhere, or stack it upside down in a corner of your garden where it will rot down into excellent garden compost. You can actually cover whatever is already there, e.g. a lawn, weeds, etc., because the weight of the material and the darkness of the membrane smothers and kills anything underneath it. (Think of the appearance of the grass on a campsite when a ground sheet has been taken away!)

Unroll the membrane and cut the first strip to length, ensuring that it is parallel to any relevant straight edge, like the edge of a path or patio, house wall, etc. The first strip should be butted well up to the edge of the site. If you are lucky you can put the edges under paving that already exists, otherwise, consider edging with bricks or slabs, because you don't want the soil underneath the membrane to trickle over the edges onto the top surface, where it will contaminate your covering material.

You can incorporate existing plants by cutting the membrane to shape around the base of the plant, rather as you would wallpaper around a light switch

Lay the gravel in a generous layer, which will anchor the membrane and smother any weed growth

You can buy special accessories for anchoring the membrane down. These range from a simple prong-like staple (like a capital E without the central bar), which come in two sizes, either 10 x 15cm (4 x 6in) or 10 x 23cm (4 x 9in). There are also a range of toothed spikes, about 15cm (6in) long (which look like Christmas trees standing on their heads), and an adhesive tape for joining the lengths together. None of these are absolutely vital, because a few old bricks or big stones will also do the trick by holding the liner down, and once the gravel is down the weight will hold the membrane firmly in place. However, you will definitely need to use them if you are covering a sloping site.

After the bed is covered in gravel, you can decorate it with rocks, containers and permanent planting

If you have a completely clear site, you can cover the whole area with horizontal strips, allowing about a 15cm (6in) overlap. If you are keeping any plants, you will have to work around these, almost as you would do in wallpapering around light switches. You will need to slit the membrane as you lay it, and then tuck the cut ends neatly around the base of the resident plants. Once you have a smooth, membrane-covered site, your gravel bed is now ready for planting up.

PLANTING SCHEMES

As always, this depends on your budget and your patience. Some people like to see plants grow and develop, others want an instant garden. See Chapters 2 and 11 for a wide choice of plants. If you use rapid-growing plants for infilling (marked R), you can thin them or remove them when the slower subjects have made sufficient growth. You can also make use of containers (see Chapter 5), to ensure a well-filled appearance until the permanent planting fills out.

You also need to plan carefully if you are preparing a bed for both hardy and half-hardy subjects. In this case, lay out the hardy plants first and make sure that there is an attractive, permanent planting which will give a good framework all the year round, with space to fill it with half-hardy material in the warmer months.

Before setting the plants arrange them loosely on the surface of the polythene until you are happy with the arrangement. As a good rule of thumb, large accent plants should be set singly to make an exclamation mark in the bed; smaller plants should follow the rule of sets of three or five. If they are set in odd-numbered clumps, this will give a well-filled arrangement that does not look too regimented. It is best to avoid even numbered clumps because they always look very blocky and unnatural.

Once you are happy with the scheme, take each plant in turn and lay it to one side of its planting position. Use a sharp knife, like a Stanley knife, or good-sized sharp scissors, to slit a large cross shape in the membrane, up to a metre (3ft) in each direction, depending, of course, on the size of the plant. Peel the four sections back on themselves, like peeling an orange, to expose the soil underneath. Dig a generous hole to accommodate the root ball with plenty of room to spare. Use sacking or surplus liner to put the excavated soil onto and drop the plant into the hole, with the junction of the soil with the plant kept at the level the plant was already at in its previous site or container.

Water the plant in well unless the ground is sodden. If your soil is heavy this is a good opportunity to improve it by adding some gravel or horticultural grit to improve drainage. You can also add granular plant food at this stage. Fill in around the root ball with some of the soil you have taken out, pushing it well in and firming the plant so that none of the roots will be in air pockets. Don't overdo the firming in, though, because air needs to get to the roots. Tamp the ground down well around the neck of the plant, then fold the membrane back and tuck it around the collar of the plant.

When all the plants have been set, dress the whole bed with up to 7.5cm (3in) depth of your chosen top dressing, though you can get away with as little as 2.5cm (1in) on a flat site. The quickest way to lay your top dressing is to use a wheelbarrow and tip out conical heaps from it at regular intervals along the strips of membrane. Then, using a really stiff broom, you can actually 'sweep' the dressing out across the membrane in a nice, even layer. However, this will only work with a dry surfacing material. The other method is to use a reversed spade, and to pull the mulch towards you in even strokes until it has been spread out over the whole surface.

The completed scheme links a pond with a living edge of succulents including *Mesembryanthemum* 'Basutoland', irises and phormiums, and a rockery planted with agaves, and echeverias

This scree bed, which has a soil composition of mainly scree and gravel, supports a contented colony of hardy *Opuntia compressa*

As far as your choice of top dressing goes, there is a much wider variety of interesting materials to choose from now, and none of it will break the bank. The cheapest material is straightforward bark chippings or cocoa shells, seashells or fine pea shingle. Along with this, there is a vast range of larger pebbles to choose from, ranging from tiny stones, through to cobbles and up to huge rounded boulders which can be used in attractive combinations. These materials have the advantages that always come from natural looking materials, in that the colours tend to be warm and harmonious.

Currently there is a boom in gardening, which has motivated vast numbers of previously uninterested people to take a new pride and enthusiasm in their gardens as an extension of their household DIY projects. This means that the huge DIY multiples have now moved into the supply of hard landscaping products on a vast scale, which has reduced the price of previously expensive materials to the level of everyone's budget. Of course, there will always be a place for the unique, higher cost, hard to source, finishes in gardens with a larger budget. For the everyday household, though, it is nice to be able to ring the changes with coloured slates, for example, available in red and blue-grey which give an interesting finish with a

reflective sheen. Gravels can be found in a rainbow variety of colours – from black, white and grey, through two-tones like black and white, and on to more dramatic red, green and blue. The smoothed glass chippings mentioned above also come in a range of frosted colours, which are bold and attractive.

There is a cornucopia of special effects available with these coloured materials, achieved by butting one type against another, but this is not for the faint-hearted. You may have seen raked Japanese gravel gardens and be entranced by the concept of a sort of 'texture lawn', with its connotations of peace and spiritual tranquillity. However, there is anything but tranquillity in store unless you are prepared to sink an edging material, like lawn edging, or to use rows of brick pavers, or other material, to keep the colours separate. Be warned! The gravel will mix and mingle and your clean edges will rapidly lose definition.

The other point with gravel is that it strays. So if you are going to use these gravelled areas as pathways to other parts of the garden, consider sinking paving stones at intervals in the through routes, to act as stepping stones. Otherwise, gravel will inevitably be walked onto adjoining surfaces. It is also uncomfortable for people wearing open-toed sandals or high heels.

Chamaecereus silvestrii var. *pectinifera* in flower makes a welcome splash of colour in this gravel bed

After a year, the gravel garden looks as if it has been there forever. *Phormium tenax 'Variegatum'* in bud in the foreground

HOW TO KEEP IT LOOKING GOOD

As already mentioned, this is low-maintenance gardening, so gravel and scree beds are very easy to care for, and are much less effort than traditional lawns and borders.

As long as you line the beds with membrane, then there is never much weeding to be done. Some weeds can get a foothold in wetter weather, when the gravel remains wet for a longer period than usual, but you will find that they are very lightly rooted because of the membrane, so they come up very easily. The site can also be sprayed with a chemical herbicide – with care. Use a sheet of cardboard, held vertically between the weeds and the plants, to protect the plants from the spray.

Other than weeding there is general housekeeping, like tidying up straggly plants. As cordylines, agaves and yuccas grow they make new leaves and the outer leaves die off. When the leaves are withered, pull them off with a really sharp, downward tug, and this will reveal the exotic trunks of the plants. Yuccas flower regularly each year, producing cream spikes of pendant, tulip-like flowers. Remove the dead flower spikes as water can accumulate in the remains during winter. You can use kitchen tongs to remove dead

petals from between the leaves, if necessary. Over time, you will need to divide up spreading plants like phormiums and the smaller succulents. This gives you new plants for using elsewhere. Look out for invasive plants that may swamp their shyer neighbours if they are not treated with a firm hand. Luckily, these invasive plants can easily be divided up, and a smaller section replanted, if required, while you will have plenty of new material for further projects. Infillers (marked R in Chapter 2) can be removed entirely or lifted and divided; again this gives you the nucleus for your next piece of exotic gardening.

Cordyline australis before removing dead leaves

Cordyline australis after removing old foliage

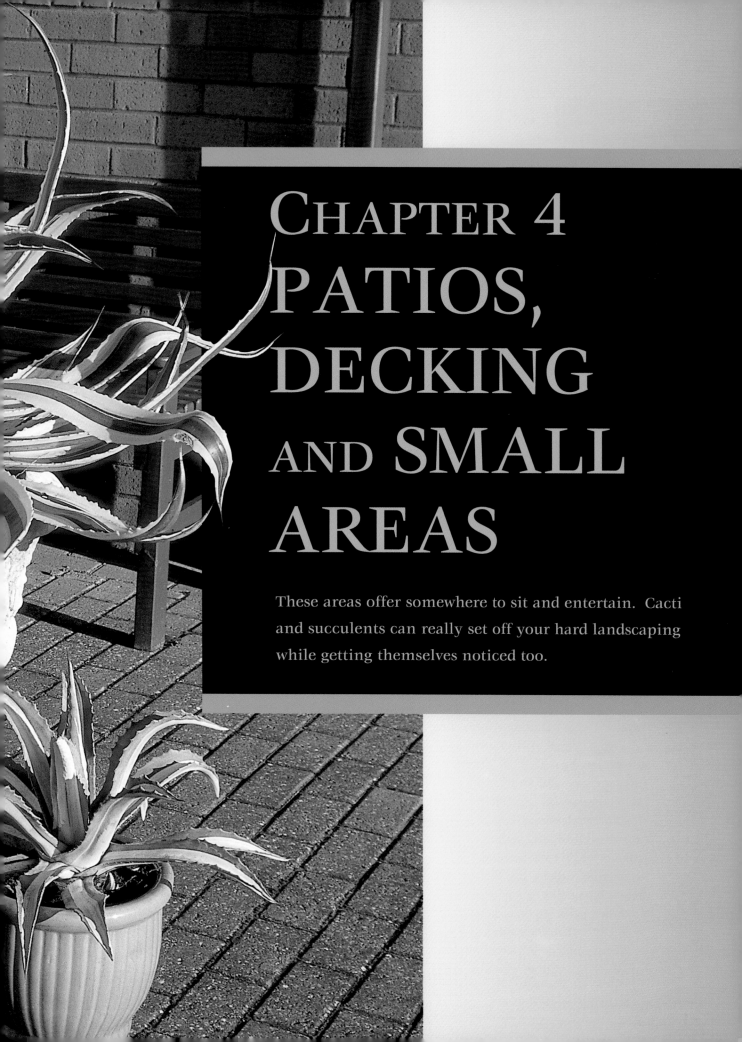

CHAPTER 4
PATIOS, DECKING AND SMALL AREAS

These areas offer somewhere to sit and entertain. Cacti and succulents can really set off your hard landscaping while getting themselves noticed too.

Yucca gloriosa 'Variegata' makes a fabulous focal point in a planting scheme, especially when it is in flower

APPLICATIONS

Many homes have an area of hard landscaping which is often the focal point of the garden, for barbecues, informal summer drinks parties and other entertaining, or as a family sitting out area. It may be a full-scale patio or area of decking, or just a small terrace or steps leading into the garden.

Plants are essential to soften the otherwise spartan appearance of large areas of hard landscaping, to bring out the colours of the materials, and to frame the whole area.

Traditional schemes can be very high maintenance. Bedding plants are lovely, but they can also be a chore. Instead of watering and deadheading after work every day, use low-maintenance, drought-resistant succulent plants instead, and come home and flop in a chair and enjoy your patio!

You can be as radical or conservative as you want. These plants fit well in a traditional paved patio, where their architectural forms make a strong impact amongst more traditional planting. They also go well with the strong colours which have become popular in gardens, like lilac or bright blue trellis or fencing, and the plants can hold their own better than their subtler relatives. You can introduce all kinds of imaginative schemes.

If you already have a traditional patio, with slabs, bricks or pavers, you can give it an instant facelift by lifting some of the slabs. This creates space for a high impact single bed planted with a cordyline (yellow, red and green *Cordyline* 'Albertii' for example), as a dramatic, architectural centrepiece. Try surrounding this exclamation point with an assortment of ground-hugging succulent plants, like sedums, saxifrages and sempervivums, or by summer bedding like pale blue pansies or greeny-white nicotiana. Or go for several small beds with single dramatic planting like the weeping, colourful rainbow phormium varieties, like 'Rainbow Maiden', for example, with its softly drooping cascade of pink leaves. Yuccas make a dramatic focal planting, the *Yucca gloriosa* 'Variegata' has striking yellow and green striped leaves and tall spires of flowers in the late summer. Or consider softly drooping *Yucca flaccida,* or its attractive cultivar *Y. flaccida* 'Golden Sword' with its

Blue-glazed pots containing *Agave americana* 'Mediopicta' and *A. americana* 'Variegata' make a very effective summer display on a patio

Trachycarpus fortunei is a striking accent plant, which looks good at every stage of its growth. It is always shapely, whether you have a small plant in a container or a large architectural centrepiece like this one

bright yellow banding. Summer bedding of black and green aeoniums, or (in the absence of children and dogs) spiky agaves are another possibility, which gives a busy feel in the summer, and a chance to ring the changes the next year when the plants need removing for winter protection.

A Japanese theme can also be attractive and, for the spiritually minded, offers a calming sanctuary. Bamboos are hardy, despite their delicate appearance, with evergreen whispering leaves. They range in height from the 4.5m (15 ft) high black canes of *Phyllostachys nigra* and the golden stemmed *Phyllostachys aurea* to the 2–3m (6½–9ft) high *Sinarundinaria nitida* with black canes and fine, dark green leaves. There is even the smaller *Pleioblastus viridistratus* 'Auricoma', with its variegated golden yellow leaves and its compact, spreading habit, growing 1–2m (3–6½ft) high. You can then add the silver and blue arching fronds of ornamental grasses, like *Carex comans* 'Frosted Curls' and

the lovely blue *Festuca glauca*, or go for the dramatic dark leaves of *Ophiopogon planiscapus* 'Nigrescens'. You can have areas of gravel amongst your paving, and rake it into patterns – sometimes a therapeutic pastime.

Or you could go for an uncompromising display of unusual plants. Try the fan-shaped leaves of *Trachycarpus fortunei* and other hardy palms for an attractive and showy permanent feature. Combine it with summer plantings of the purple-black rosettes of *Aeonium arboreum* 'Zwartkop' contrasted with the lime green of *A. arboreum, or A. arboreum* 'Variegatum' or zebra striped *Agave americana* 'Variegata' with its bright yellow and green spiky rosettes. Many aloes form trunks in time, like *Aloe ferox* and *A. gariepensis* mentioned previously in Chapter 2. See also *Aloe davyana,* which is olive green with whitish markings.

SITING

By their nature, sitting-out areas tend to be close to the house, with all the advantages that go with this, like borrowed heat, and the shelter of walls and angles of the house, which extends the range of planting available and also gives a good background to the plants.

The plants will benefit from the same factors that influence the siting of these areas for the comfort of their human residents. If you are constructing an area from scratch, look for the same features that apply to siting the gravel and scree beds of Chapter 3. South– or southwest-facing, sunny, sheltered and wind-proofed areas suit both people and the plants. Occasionally, if a house is situated in a very shady position, people are forced to consider siting a patio or terrace at the opposite end of the garden, in effect rotating it to catch the sun. Your plants will appreciate this, too, though you will need to think long and hard about the drawbacks of trekking backwards and forwards with food and drink if you are the main cook and bottlewasher!

CONSTRUCTION

Every garden, even the smallest, needs some sort of hard landscaped area for sitting out and for access to the garden on wetter days; in fact the smallest garden can be all hard landscape with a planted courtyard effect. The amount of work even the most modest-sized lawn can create has to be considered very carefully, especially when there is such a range of economically priced products to choose from in the multi-outlet DIY stores and garden centres.

There are four main factors to consider: what surface you will use, the use to which the area is to be put, the appearance and your overall budget.

PAVED AREAS
Flexible surfacing uses loose materials such as the gravel already covered in the previous

This patio has been constructed in a sunny position away from the shadows of house walls. Large *Trachycarpus fortunei* give shade, while other plants in containers soften the hard lines of the paving

chapter, but it also includes any surface which allows a degree of movement, including block paving, sets, and bricks which are loose laid in sand, with a dry mortar mix brushed between the joints. Flexible surfacing creates fewer problems with drainage and cracking and does not need such deep foundations, although weed invasion may cause problems unless some sort of liner is incorporated.

Paving comes in a plethora of colours including these pink riven slabs

Rigid surfaces are ones which do not have this built in flexibility; this means surfaces like a solid raft of concrete, or slabs and paving bedded into mortar over a rigid foundation of compacted hard core or concrete. Care needs to be taken with materials – too thin and brittle and they can shift or crack – and care needs to be taken to ensure that surface water drains away. These surfaces are less amenable to any change of heart you may have; removal is a real problem, which is to be avoided as far as possible.

As far as appearance goes, you have the choice of matching the paving as near as possible to the materials from which your house is constructed, or of going for a contrast. Natural stone is the most expensive and aesthetically appealing, but there are so many artificially produced paving slabs that look good and won't break the bank that there is something for every budget. You can also buy ready-made features, like paving slabs with cut out centres to frame a specimen plant.

Although harmony has been *de rigueur* in gardening, if you want to be really different then go for it! Don't be afraid to stick your neck out and go for a really dramatic look if you are brave enough. Today, patios in particular are treated as outside rooms and

unusual colours and materials are becoming commonplace. If you have gone for eye-watering colour inside then there is no good reason to stop at the patio door. Exterior paints come in mouth-watering shades such as blues, purples and terracotta. Match them with painted garden furniture and bring out cheerful tablecloths and seat cushions when you are entertaining. Be brave and try metallic finishes.

Surface texture is important, and not just for its visual qualities. Natural materials like York Stone can become very slippery, while artificial 'riven' surfaces come in a range of colours from grey and buff to pinker and bluer choices and have a non-slip surface. You can always mix materials – on a paved patio infilling odd areas with cobbles or brick instead of paving can look attractive, and don't forget to leave space for planting.

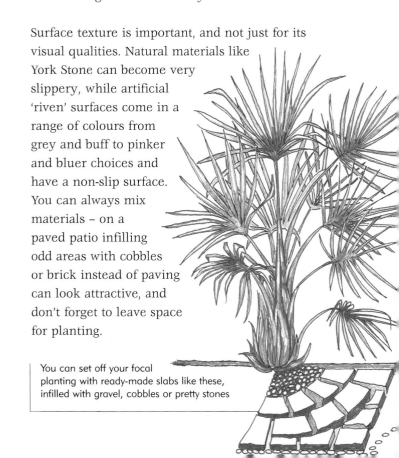

You can set off your focal planting with ready-made slabs like these, infilled with gravel, cobbles or pretty stones

In every case, for a paved area you will need a level site with a base of well-compacted soil, and hard core or concrete for the foundations. You can also construct a moveable patio, if you haven't decided on a fixed area, or if you feel that you are likely to want to ring the changes on a regular basis.

In the example photographed, the area had already been prepared for use as a gravel bed. This meant that the surface was already level and lined with permeable membrane topped with a good layer of pea shingle. In the photographs you can see the gravel in the patio is being given a final levelling within the marked up area that the patio is intended to cover. The surface is then smoothed in sweeping arcs with a large straight-edged board, which is swept across the whole surface to even out any irregularities. A straight edge is placed in position along the length of the first edge of the patio, and the slabs are carefully lowered into position, then butted up to one another before dropping each one into place and levelled with an overall tapping from a hammer shaft.

This method also works for the decking 'tiles', which create an instant surface for sitting out and enjoying the weather and your garden.

A level gravel base is being prepared for a layer of patio slabs. The gravel is being levelled with a large, straight-edged board

Final smoothing of the gravel is done by making sweeping arcs with the wooden board

Use the board to provide a straight edge to line up the paving slabs

Slopes can, of course, be accommodated by terracing, but in effect, each terraced area has the same basic requirements as a normal level patio. On a sloping site a raised patio overlooking a garden that falls away can make for an interesting change of level and perspective, and you have the decorative effect of a step or steps to edge with pots or planting. Conversely a garden can drop down to a paved area against the house with descending steps – drainage is a particularly important consideration in this case.

The slabs are carefully levelled by tapping them with an inverted hammer

The final patio is complete. It now has a small wall and houses a pretty park bench and several containers of plants

You can make an instant decking, using wooden tiles, which are readily available from DIY outlets

ventilation and drainage. In all cases the wood should be thoroughly treated against damp and decay, but particularly in the case of suspended decking which could cause a bad accident if the wood gave away. Don't forget that the bolts need to be weather resistant too; there have been accidents caused by the bolts decaying which is just as disastrous even if the wood is perfectly sound.

Do consider access before covering your whole garden with raised wooden decks – it can make a convenient home for mice, rats and other vermin.

If you like the look of decking but you do not want the expense and effort of full decking construction, you can now buy decking tiles which can be laid directly onto an old patio, or bedded into a gravel base. They look really convincing and save an awful lot of hard work! They come in a variety of finishes and you have the choice of laying them with all the straight edges running parallel to one another, or in a criss cross pattern instead.

WOODEN DECKING

Wooden decking has become popular and DIY chains offer kits to construct a decking area with a minimum of cost and effort. However, decking has some drawbacks. Decking has a Californian ambience of dry, sunny days: in damper climates wooden surfaces can become extremely slippery when wet. In the winter months a build up of moss and algae can create a skating rink, so you should consider a textured surface. Chicken wire is functional for grip, though ugly.

Decking can be laid on sleepers across a solid base (like an old and unsightly concrete patio), or can be constructed across a timber framework raised above ground level for

USE OF UNUSUAL MATERIALS

As touched upon above, consider setting off the plants with unusual materials from the garden centre. As well as interspersing paving with cobbles and bricks, consider shells, river-moulded pebbles, (but use your garden centres rather than raiding local beaches) or a mosaic made from broken tiles. Below the Parc de Attraccions on the northeastern slopes of Montjuic in Barcelona is the Mirador del Alcalde, which is a fabulous viewpoint which gives a panorama of Barcelona, framed by a profusion of *Agave americana* 'Variegata' and kniphofia (red hot pokers).

But don't forget to look down at what you are standing on. The paving is made up of all sorts

Inspirational use of scrap materials in paving at the Mirador del Alcalde, Barcelona, Spain

of scrap materials which have been inlayed into the ground in patterns. There is a variety of concrete pipes, transmission chains, cutlery, mechanical parts and loads of old screws, washers, cogs, etc., plus the necks and bases of bottles. All of these ideas could present an interesting challenge for those with the time and enough of the raw material. The bottles are set upside down into cement, with the dimpled bases showing in a glittery mosiac.

Look too at sculptural effects. There is a wider variety of cheaper statues than

ever before from the winsome to the classical. These can look very effective and are affordable by just about everyone. Found objects – like river-rounded boulders, quarried rocks, old logs and driftwood also look very sympathetic. And don't forget the architectural finds – like chimney pots, drainage pipes etc.

If you are planting into spaces left by slabs lifted out of the patio, or in areas of soil alongside your patio, it is worth spending some time turning the soil over, incorporating some new top soil if the soil is particularly exhausted. This is also a good opportunity to ensure that the soil is well-drained by adding extra drainage material, like pea shingle, horticultural grit or sharp sand if it is particularly heavy.

Raised beds or double-walls give particularly good conditions for drought-resistant plants like these, where their thirstier cousins could never survive. See Chapter 7, Unusual Rockeries, for information on constructing a variety of raised beds.

Succulents enjoy the benefits of a free-draining raised bed. This planting, of half-hardy echeverias, is set off with a dressing of blue slate chippings, which are a pale blue-grey when dry, turning a deep glossy navy when wet

PLANTING SCHEMES

Again you need to decide whether you will be using all hardy, or a hardy/half-hardy mixture of plants.

Scale is important. With your hardy selections, for height look at palms and cordylines, which are relatively slow growing and their fine root systems are much less of a threat to foundations than more traditional subjects. However, even with slower-growing subjects like these, think carefully about the height and spread as you want to avoid making interior rooms dark when plants grow up. *Trachycarpus fortunei* is slow growing but the huge fronds do cover a surprisingly wide circle – it would be a shame to have to cut back such a special choice, so in this case think perhaps of *Chaemerops humilis*, a smaller-growing, yet equally hardy palm. *Brahea armata* is also slow growing, and will stand a lot of frost.

Also, as you tend to be sitting amongst these plants rather than using them more for a landscape effect to look out on, you can look at the subtleties of form and structure, and unusual colours. Some of the rosette-forming plants are particularly sympathetic, such as the agaves, the phormiums and some of the grasses.

On raised areas such as walls and raised beds, you can look at the hardy sedums, saxifrages and sempervivums, all of which can stay in position and will scramble attractively. Because these are drought-resistant plants, you can push little bits into

This patio corner is furnished with interesting container plants that can be changed around whenever you want. From l to r, *Cycas revoluta, Echeveria subrigida, Cotyledon orbiculata, Euphobia cooperi* and *Sedum frutescens*

A stone planter containing *Sedum sieboldii* f. *variegatum, Pitcairnia ferruginea* and *Graptopetalum pentandrum* subsp. *superbum*

gaps in walls and paving slabs where they will take hold readily and glow like little jewels. Sempervivum-like jovibarbas are useful. Look, too, at *Orostachys spinosas* with its yellow flowers and grey-green rosettes – reminiscent of miniature green sunflower heads. Other orostachys are also worth planting. Lewisias will flower profusely in the spring. They have flat rosettes of dark green leaves and bear numerous and long-lived flowers in shades of white, pink and red.

Sempervivums can be planted into crevices in stone walls, and other inhospitable places. These are growing happily in a chunk of volcanic rock

Half-hardy choices include the rosette-forming aloes. You can also consider the unusual and lovely half-hardy trailing succulents, like *Crassula pellucida* subsp. *marginalis* and *Senecio rowleyanus* (string of beads). You can also try *Senecio herreianus,* an interesting trailing plant which is good for hanging baskets, and which has green bead-like leaves with translucent lines and white flowers. *Sedum morganianum* (donkey's tail) and the silver and green sprays of *S. sieboldii* f. *variegatum* are other attractive species, plus echeverias, with their mouth-watering colours, can make very attractive beds, and are so colourful that they are almost flowers in their own right.

A cactus bed makes an unusual arrangement, and can stay planted out all year if you choose all hardy subjects (see Chapter 2). Watch out for spines if you have small children and set the plants well back from inquisitive fingers. It's also important to consider trimming the spikes off agaves in sitting-out areas, as the leaves have points that can be fierce, and the plants do not seem to suffer at all for trimming back.

Low-growing, carpeting succulents go well in paving slabs and again will spill down walls and soften the edges of steps.

HOW TO KEEP IT LOOKING GOOD

Don't let invasive weeds get a foothold amongst the creeping succulents. A small amount of regular weeding will save hours of work in future. Make sure you keep an eye on plants growing side by side, or you may find one has been smothered by its greedy neighbour. Be ruthless with plants that are growing too big or losing their shape, and don't be afraid to cut them back, or divide them up.

Trailing plants can be increased very readily; nip out the growing points to bush up the growth; if you nip out longer pieces, push them back into the soil alongside the parent plants when they will root rapidly.

Sempervivum rosettes die after flowering, but don't worry. A new baby plant or plants will usually be coming up alongside the parent.

Above all, always be prepared for happy accidents; left to their own devices – but not allowed to run wild – many of these plants will insinuate themselves across paving slabs, up walls, etc., which often looks much prettier than a more contrived or manicured look.

A reproduction lead urn, containing *Agave americana* 'Variegata', makes an austere statement on this formal patio

STONE SINK REPLICAS

Glazed sinks can be disguised very effectively as stone sink replicas. Clean the sink really well, and make sure it is grease free. Coat the surface of the sink with a multipurpose adhesive, continuing the adhesive over the rim of the sink and down to below the ultimate soil level.

Mix two parts of multipurpose compost with one part of fine horticultural grit or sharp sand and one part cement. Mix with water until you have a fairly thick mixture and apply it to the tacky surfaces of the sink. You can leave the finish exactly as it is, or you can wait until it begins to harden and then you can mark the surface with indentations and irregularities for authenticity.

Toilets can take the same treatment too, if you want a conversation piece, and if you can quell your imagination enough to try it out! You can also use this mixture to construct mock stone sinks and containers.

First find two cardboard boxes which will fit one inside the other with about a 7.5cm (3in) gap between them. Line the inside of the first box with cling film, and cover the outside of the second one with a layer of the same material. Take the larger, empty cling film-lined box and pour the mock stone mixture into the bottom making up a layer of around 7.5cm (3in) deep. Stand the second box inside the first on top of the mixture and pour the remaining mixture down the gaps between the two boxes until the 'walls' reach the height you require. Wait for the mixture to set, remove your cardboard box inner and outer moulds and you have a nice 'stone' container for a fraction of the cost of the real thing. Because of the compost in the mixture, the colour and finish is very sympathetic and you will find that it quickly weathers naturally and attractively.

This stone corner pot houses a pretty assortment of sempervivums

SITING

Siting is not really an issue because all cacti
and other succulents will be happy more or
less anywhere but in dankest, sopping wet
shade. All the awkward areas in strong sunlight
are perfect for containers, which are also
happy in the problem dry spots, like paving,
steps, drive and path edges and around front
doors. However, they will also sit happily out
of sight in shadier areas when you want to ring
the changes and you can slip them in and out
of position as and when they look their best, or
when you fancy a new look.

You can put containers out of harm's way of
children. You can also protect little fingers and
pets' noses from your spikier subjects by
strategic positioning when they are around.
And you can avoid damage to your precious
favourites during ball games, or if parties spill
outside, or the gathering round the barbecue
gets a bit over-excited on long summer
evenings.

masonry drill and don't forget eye protection,
in case fragments fly up. You can get cheap
plastic goggles from DIY outlets.

As an added protection, especially if you are
heavy-handed with the watering can, drainage
material should be added to the bottom of the
pot; either broken crocks, pebbles or – an ideal
lightweight solution – polystyrene packing
material. This is apparently indestructible and
makes for a much more portable container,
though it is a really tiresome material to
handle as it clings to clothes and swirls off
around the garden on the slightest current of
air. Choose a still day.

Any proprietary soil-based (John Innes)
compost, or non-soil-based multipurpose
compost will do, with the addition of a little
granular feed if you are not planning to replant
the container for some time. Again, it may be
worth adding sharp sand or horticultural grit to
make a nice, free-draining mixture.

CONSTRUCTION

Construction is straightforward, but containers
for succulent plants do need drainage holes if
your plants are not to succumb to being too
wet – which is a pleasant reverse to the
insatiability of normal, more water-guzzling,
plants.

Succulent containers must dry out between
watering, as these plants do not have the same
resistance to rots and moulds that their
relatives originating in wetter areas have
developed. In fact, you can really only kill
them by excessive kindness.

It is only a moment's work to drill drainage
holes if they aren't already there, and it is
courting disaster if you don't do so. Use a

These containers will seldom need watering,
though they will appreciate a drink in the
driest periods (about once a week), and will
also enjoy feeding with a fertilizer formulated
for tomatoes if you find the time.

Materials for planting up a container consisting of equal
amounts of John Innes No. 3 and sharp gravel, plus
rocks for drainage in the bottom, and ornamental rocks
for decoration

Grouping a genus together in containers can look very effective, like these cordylines

Hardy subjects can stay outside all the year round and many make an attractive and colourful evergreen winter display. Remember to keep half-hardy subjects in a frost-free place; either as a display in the house or conservatory, or out of sight in a dry garage or outhouse if you prefer – though this is a pity unless you simply cannot squeeze them in anywhere.

In the growing season, you will need to tidy the pots up. Pinch out straggly bits, and remove dead lower leaves. Nip back trailing plants to thicken out the growth, as the cut ends will sprout several new heads. Don't forget to keep the pieces you remove. If you dry them off for a few days to ensure that the cut edges are calloused over, and then push them into the pots alongside their parents, they will root very readily which, again, will result in a more generous display.

HOW TO KEEP THEM LOOKING GOOD

These pots will reward you for a very long time, because they retain their good looks year on year and they need very little care. Plants in section A will all stand neglect but when they are planted up in containers they will appreciate weekly watering in the growing season, especially in hot, dry spells. If growth is your priority, many of the succulents appreciate extra watering and feeding in the growing season; plants like agaves, for example, will grow into strapping specimens more rapidly with more generous watering and feeding. Plants in section B need regular watering in containers. Bamboos, in particular, are high-maintenance plants in containers as they are very, very thirsty!

Succulents make easy-care and low-maintenance plants for window boxes. In the larger container from l to r, *Aloe ferox*, *Aeonium arboreum* and *Aloe gariepensis*. The smaller one contains, from l to r, *Echeveria subsessilis*, *Agave filifera* and *Echeveria* 'Perle von Nurnberg'

CHAPTER 6
POOLS AND WATER FEATURES

Succulents make wonderful living carpets of evergreen foliage, often studded with flowers, which will clothe the edges of ponds, while spiky architecturals look fabulous mirrored in the water.

Spiky yuccas contrast well with the softer edging of succulents around this pond

APPLICATIONS

For many people a garden would not be complete without some kind of water feature, ranging from a large pond with a rockery waterfall or a fountain to a smaller feature, like a millstone or a lion's head on a wall, with water trickling onto stones. Water gives so much added interest to a garden, offering reflections, sounds and a focal point. There is almost nothing more relaxing than sitting and listening to the trickle or splash of moving water on a sultry hot day and, just as a fire in a house acts as a magnet for people to sit around, so does a pond in the garden.

One of the problems that results from the creation of an artificial pond is finding an effective camouflage for the pond edges. Succulent plants can solve the problem because they form dense and compact mats so they can be chosen and planted up as a wonderful living carpet. They offer a variety of textures, shapes and colours and because

many of the plants are evergreen, they can offer you an all-the-year-round solution, to an attractive clothing for the pond edges.

SITING A POND

Try to find a good open position, well away from any overhanging trees. Any pond is happier without a sludge of rotting, fallen leaves which look unsightly and make the water stagnant. Furthermore, when you are planting around the pond with plants like cacti and succulents, and other drought-resistant choices, they, too, will be happier in a well-lit position.

Your next decision is what type of pond you are looking for. You will need to consider whether you prefer a formal or informal water garden. A formal geometrical shape, like a square, rectangle, oval or circle really needs an equally formal, geometrical setting to see it at its best. Is the pond going to be sunken in the ground or are you planning to have a raised pool with a wall of bricks or railway sleepers?

Irregular, more natural, shapes lend themselves to a less contrived setting. Here, in effect, you are suggesting that you have a little piece of nature, which has been parcelled up and transplanted into a garden setting. You are aiming for the illusion of a natural water feature, be it pond, a section of stream, a

Nestled in a bed of *Sedum album* 'Coral Carpet', this water feature creates a soothing sound and acts as a magnet when sitting out in the summer

spring, waterfall over a rocky outcrop or whatever. Of course, unless you are lucky enough to have natural water features, the whole thing is completely artificial, and the illusion takes time, effort and money.

Once you have picked your shape, you need to consider whether you are having fully paved edges with an overhang to cover the liner. Paving, in this context, means the use of any hard edging material, which can, of course, include decking. Paving slabs, or rocks and stones can be placed at intervals around the pond edge, with planting in between the gaps. Or you can go for a scheme that uses plants alone as a living edge.

Unless you are constructing a huge landscape feature, the pond is best situated near the house or near a sitting-out area so that you can enjoy the sight and sound of it. Ideally, go for a position where the feature is visible both from indoors and outdoors. Unless you have a raised site with vantage points, it's also important to have the pond running at an angle to the line of sight, so that the water is actually visible. A rectangle or an oval shaped pond with its longer edge parallel with the line of sight will actually be more or less invisible until you are on top of it, which can be incredibly disappointing. So do spend some time planning the shape. Laying lengths of rope to shape in situ can give you a good idea of how the pond will look, and you will find that they often look much smaller than you imagine. As with a rockery, in general the best advice is to go for the largest pond you can afford.

Look at landscaping the whole area. Water features harmonize very sympathetically with many other garden features discussed in this book, like gravel and scree beds, patios and decking, and rockeries.

This rockery and waterfall is planted with phormium, agave and echeveria and leads to a pond with a living edge of succulents

And don't forget, the whole thing is an illusion, so feel free to fake things. A large-budget water feature with conjoined pools connected by streams is a wonderful though costly sight. If you want the illusion without the cost of extra liner, large pumps etc. you can create the impression of two ponds linked by a connecting stream, or imply that a stream meanders into your existing pond. A gravel bed can be created with a meandering channel running through it, lined with a 'dry stream bed' of river or sea-smoothed rocks and boulders. This gives the effect of a landscape with a stream without the actual effort and expense. Ironically, after a torrential fall of rain during a summer storm, our pond did actually overflow along the 'river bed', taking one rather fat and confused Mirror carp with it, which then had to be retrieved from amongst the pebbles. This mock stream is discussed more fully in Chapter 7, next, on Unusual Rockeries.

CONSTRUCTION

A) THE POND

Concrete ponds have fallen out of favour, as they are difficult to construct and maintain because they have a tendency to shift and crack, causing problems with leaks. This topic is beyond the scope of this book, and the real choice, therefore, is between buying a pre-cast pool in resin or fibreglass, or choosing a flexible liner. There is a tremendous range of liners, which have a life span of up to 20 to 25 years. As stated previously, rather as with a rockery, go for the biggest liner or pre-formed pool you can afford. Not only because you might find that the completed pond looks disappointingly small (and, of course, it is cheaper to make one pond a bit bigger than to end up with two which you will probably then want to connect up) but also because it is much easier to achieve a natural balance, with healthy plants and fish and pure water, in a larger pool.

A pond has to be at least 0.5m (20in) deep if you hope to populate it with a colony of fish that can survive the winter. Because they are cold-blooded, fish survive because their metabolic rate slows right down until it just ticks over until the warmer weather arrives. However, they need sufficient depth in the pond to be able to lurk at the bottom, in a kind of suspended animation. In a shallow pond there is always the danger that all of the water will freeze.

You can see straight away what you are getting when you look at the pre-formed shapes available in garden centres. However, if you are going to buy a liner, you will need to have decided on the ultimate size of your intended pond, and to

have calculated the liner size you need to construct this in advance.

Again, this is easy arithmetic, but do double check it before the liner is actually cut off the roll; mistakes could be costly! To calculate the liner size that you will have to buy, take the maximum length and maximum width of your projected pond. To each of these dimensions, add the maximum depth multiplied by two plus an extra 0.6m (24in) to allow for a 30cm (1ft) overlap on each side. Therefore for a pond which is 2.5m (8ft) long by 1.8m (6ft) wide with a depth of 0.5m (20in) you would require a liner which is 4m (12ft) x 3.5m (11ft), calculated as follows:

Metric:
Length: 2.5m (0.5m x 2) + 0.6m, which is 2.5 + 1 + 0.6m = total 4.1m
Width: 1.8m + (0.5m x 2) + 0.6m, which is 1.8 + 1 + 0.6m = total 3.4m

Imperial:
Length: 8ft + (1½ft x 2) + 2ft, which is 8ft + 3ft + 2ft = total 13ft
Width: 6ft + (1½ft x 2) + 2ft, which is 6ft + 3ft + 2ft = total 11ft

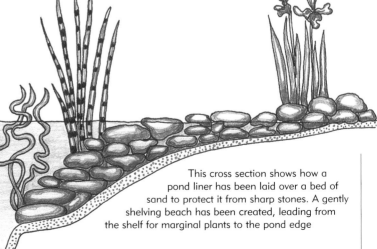

This cross section shows how a pond liner has been laid over a bed of sand to protect it from sharp stones. A gently shelving beach has been created, leading from the shelf for marginal plants to the pond edge

Sedum pachyclados and saxifraga edge this pond, which also provides a home for frogs, newts and goldfish

Dig out the pond, allowing for a shelf all around of about 30cm (1ft) deep, for marginal plants to stand on. It is also easier for frogs and newts to get in and out, and you will find that pools generally act as a magnet for wild birds to bathe in and drink from. They can drown quickly and easily in a sheer-sided deep pool. You can always add an area of stones and pebbles to act as a gently shelving beach, connecting the marginals' shelf to the pond edge, for added protection for wildlife.

For stability of the structure, the sides need to shelve at an angle of about 45 degrees. Anything steeper has a tendency to slide inwards. After you have dug the shape out, check with a spirit level to ensure that the horizontal surfaces are level. This is essential. Otherwise the water surface will never be horizontal and you will never be happy with it.

If your site is stony, remove any visible rocks and sharp stones that might puncture the liner and line the hole with commercial underliner, old carpets or a layer of soft builders' sand a good 2.5cm (1in) deep to give a soft and protective surface. Lay the liner in the hole, draping it loosely over the internal shape, and peg it down with stones. Fill the pool with a hose pipe, when the pressure of the water will iron out the wrinkles in the liner and mould the edges to the pool's internal dimensions.

If you are using a pre-formed liner, dig a hole to roughly the correct dimensions and line it with sand. The pre-cast liner then has a yielding surface to bed itself into. Again, use a spirit level to make sure that the pool is sitting horizontally, and infill with soil around the sides. To ensure that the pressure is equalized on the inside and outside of the shape, you need to shovel the soil in around the pool edges while it is filling.

A living pond edge of carpeting succulents with a spiky architectural backdrop of yuccas and phormiums

Vigorous-growing *Sedum pachyclados,* saxifraga and cushion-forming *Scleranthus biflorus* will completely cover the pond liner in no time

You can use one of the following for the edges:

i) Soil. This has to finish slightly back and away from the actual liner edge or it will tumble in and foul the water. Heap the soil in a wedge shape, with the narrowest edge nearest to the water, and with the soil increasing in depth as it tapers backwards from the pond edge.

When you come to set plants, set them in the deeper soil furthest away from the edge. This will stabilise the pond edges because the roots will knit the soil together. You will find that the plants will automatically grow towards the water. You have to have faith at this point, because the whole thing will look very stark initially with the exposed liner edges. However, although the plants will, of course, grow in all directions they will actually grow more lushly at the water's edge once they reach it, as they will get plenty to drink there.

ii) A mixture of soil and rocks, slabs or cobbles. Again, the soil should take up the shape of a wedge in cross-section.

iii) Solid edges. You can use one of the huge ranges of paving slabs, decking etc., laid so that there is a sufficient overhang to cover the unsightly edges of the liner. An alternative is to alter the profile of the pond as you dig it out. Instead of a marginals' shelf with a 45-degree slope to the water's edge, as described above, you can add a very shallow sloping lip down into the pond, like an imperceptibly shelving beach, with the liner continuing up to cover the slope. This gently shelving liner-covered slope is then filled from above water level and continuing down to below the water surface, with an assortment of boulders, cobbles and pebbles. This looks natural and attractive, and allows for a range of planting around the pool and in the water margins.

There are also a couple of low-cost cheats for you to try if you are on a budget:

iv) Mock stone edges. You can use old newspaper soaked in a cement mixture to form a very natural-looking 'papier-mache' edging, with hollows for plants created as the edge is formed. This is messy but cheap and very effective. You cannot add fish to a pond edged like this for some weeks, until the lime in the cement has leached away. Mix a fairly sloppy solution of sand, water and cement, and dunk sheets of newspaper into this until they are sodden. You can mould the resulting materials into as many forms as your imagination can come up with. One option is to build an edge up on the actual liner/soil margin; the other is to create polythene-lined moulds, as described in v), below.

v) You can construct lightweight mock rocks for the pond edging, again with pre-formed hollows for planting, using a mixture of one part cement to two parts multi-purpose compost to three parts soft (builders') sand.

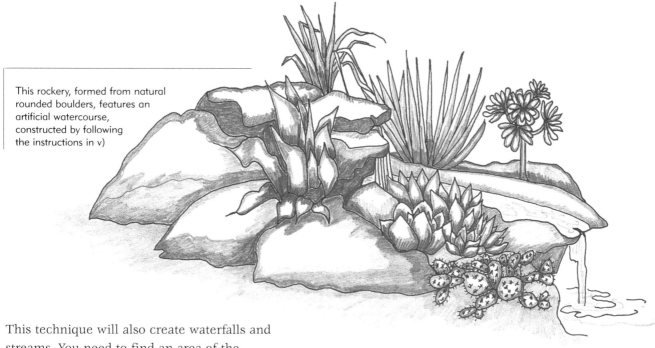

This rockery, formed from natural rounded boulders, features an artificial watercourse, constructed by following the instructions in v)

This technique will also create waterfalls and streams. You need to find an area of the garden where you can dig out the moulds for your rocks and streams. These holes are lined with polythene, and long narrow shapes, like streams, have to be reinforced with a layer of chicken wire. These create incredibly naturalistic rocks and streams, as you can see in the photograph below. The best cheat is to mix the artificial rocks with natural rock; then dare anyone to guess which is which. You need to plan ahead with this, as these rocks and features are also toxic to fish until the chemical compounds have dissipated. The watercourse in the photograph below was buried for a whole winter; this meant we had a ready-weathered and very convincing stream to install the next spring.

An artificial boulder covered in *Mesembryanthemum* 'Basutoland'

This watercourse is a homemade cheat, constructed as described in section v)

B) MOVING WATER

A pond isn't a pond without moving water. There is a massive choice of fantastic water features, ranging from classical nymphs with urns, to rumbustious pigs frolicking in jacuzzies! Waterfalls lend themselves to the more naturalistic pond, cascading down a series of rocky outcrops. Fountains evoke a more formal world and suit a formal setting though, of course, rules are made to be broken.

Unless you are a really keen DIY-er, there are so many ready-made kits available that it is really easy to go out and pick up and create the whole structure in a weekend. However, there is one big proviso. Electricity and water are a potentially lethal combination and although perfectly safe fountains and water falls can be constructed, you need weather-proof electrical installation, plus circuit breakers, and you might prefer to use a transformer to step down the voltage. If in doubt, CONSULT AN ELECTRICIAN. There is also a new generation of solar-powered fountains which work without the need for mains electricity.

C) STAND–ALONE WATER FEATURES

If you don't want the hassle of maintaining a pond, or if you have vulnerable small children, there are many water features without a pond. (Don't forget that a toddler can drown in a couple of inches of water and that water draws them like a magnet.) In this case, a reservoir of water in a sunken plastic tank, topped with a grating or cover camouflaged with rocks or pre-formed features, like millstones, can give you all the pleasure of the sight and sound of running water without the upkeep. Again, consult an electrician, unless you are 100 per cent sure that you can install the pump and wiring safely yourself.

PLANTING SCHEMES

Carpeting succulents offer a dream solution to the problem of covering up ugly pond liners. They create a colourful, evergreen living edge to your pool, which will cover every scrap of liner and drip over into the water itself.

In the pond keep to your architectural theme with rushes, sedges, and irises, which have the benefit of producing dramatic spiky foliage and a wide range of colourful flowers. At the damp edges of the pond itself you can cheat a little and go for spiky acorus. They are not true ornamental grasses but they are grass-like, with flattened fans of dark green leaves. Because they enjoy damp conditions they are very good for pond sides. Look out for *Acorus gramineus* 'Variegatus', which is a hardy, perennial, semi-evergreen, with dark green and cream variegated arching foliage, reaching a height of 25cm (10in) and with a spread of 15cm (6in). *Acorus gramineus* 'Hakuro-nishiki', is another good choice, this

Yucca gloriosa 'Variegata' and *Phormium* 'Yellow Wave' frame this fountain and statue

CHAPTER 7
UNUSUAL ROCKERIES

Cacti and succulents make an interesting change from
traditional rockery plants, and they will also thrive
in the well-drained conditions.

APPLICATIONS

The traditional rockery has always had a place close to the heart of every gardener. It combines the appeal of landscape in miniature with a choice environment for plants that are often more difficult to grow. On a flat site, it creates changes of level. On a sloping site, combined with zigzag paths, slopes or steps, it is a method of coping aesthetically with a plot that is sometimes awkward to manage.

Cacti and succulents, along with other architectural plants, offer an interesting alternative to the traditional rockery and they lend themselves especially well to this situation. On the whole, the plants are less vigorous so the rockery stays under control more easily than when it is planted with more rampant, carpeting choices. The raised, free-draining position also suits the plants very well, and cacti and succulents can sometimes be grown in a rockery in a less than favourable geographical position when they would surely perish if they were planted directly into the level ground.

You can use cacti and succulents for a radically different and somewhat minimalist planting scheme, or succulent, carpeting plants if you prefer a busier, well-filled look. The plants will also mix well together with careful planting, or they can make surprising or subtle additions to your existing rockery whether it is planted with alpines, miniature bulbs, dwarf conifers or any of these in combination.

There are also a variety of 'alternative' rockeries which you can try, apart from the traditional form which mimics a natural rocky outcrop.

SITING

Because cacti and succulents like a well-drained position, rockeries offer almost ideal conditions, and, as stated above, in less favourable areas of Britain, are perhaps the only way that these plants can safely be treated as hardy.

It is interesting to take a look at how plants actually grow in their habitat or in an adopted habitat where they have become naturalized. *Agave americana*, for example, are ubiquitous plants, growing like weeds on the cliffs of the Spanish Costa Brava. Their ideal location, where they grow large and flower prolifically, is on almost vertical rock faces, where water will drain quickly from the more vulnerable inner leaves. This gives a clue for treatment of more marginally hardy plants here, and all of the rosette-shaped forms from agaves, down to lewisias will survive more readily on a sloping site.

A raised, sloping, well-drained site is ideal for these plants. Ideally a sunny, south-facing slope is the first choice, preferably with some shelter from the wind and perhaps a light background to reflect the sun. The tenderest

These sempervivums are thriving in this unusual tree stump planter

Echeveria glauca is happy in this sunny spot, where the rocks give it shelter from the weather

A good traditional rockery involves using rocks from one family bedded in as though they are running along the original rock strata. The implication is that the rocks continue under the ground as though they are part of a natural hillside, with only the weathered portions where the rocks have been exposed visible. Even on its smallest scale, with an almost flat bed constructed from a series of overlapping slabs of slate or sandstone, the illusion of an underlying geographical feature needs to be maintained.

When constructing a stratified rockery bury between a third and half of each of the rocks in the ground for stability

subjects can be given extra protection if they are tucked into the shelter of an overhanging rock for protection, and they should also be planted in the steepest, most vertical position that you can give them.

CONSTRUCTION

i) STRATIFIED ROCK OUTCROPS

This is the rockery that most people visualize, with stepped terraces of rocks interspersed with crevices for planting up. For economy there is a temptation to use any bits and pieces that have accumulated in the garden over the years, including broken paving slabs and lumps of concrete and brick. Unfortunately, this begins by looking bitty and unconvincing and continues in exactly the same way, hence its scathing nickname of dog's cemetery.

This stratified rockery is ready for planting. Notice how the rocks are tilted backwards and downwards for stabilty and to ensure some water will run to the plant roots

York stone is one of the most attractive and durable materials for a rockery. It often has attractive markings from the river sediment laid down in it when it first formed

York stone is one of the best materials for a long-lasting rockery. It stands up to frost over a period of years and has an attractive, mellow golden tone. Limestone, though a traditional choice, has a shorter life span because water will permeate the minute fractures in the stones, freeze in the winter, and cause internal cracking which will eventually lead to flaking and splitting. Rain is also damaging to limestone. It is slightly acidic and it will therefore slowly eat away at the alkaline limestone (hence the caves, potholes and other underground water systems of the limestone areas of the Peak District of northern central England). Gypsum, although it is a fabulous, glittery pale material, which makes stark and dramatic garden features, is also, sadly, relatively short-lived.

Ideally, choose the largest rocks that you can obtain, afford and, importantly, move when you get them on site. Unfortunately, because the quantity of rocks involved is so large, this can mean that a rockery is an expensive operation. In the interests of conservation, you should source the materials from a reputable quarry or garden centre, and there has to be a certain minimum scale for a scheme like this to look effective. The cheapest method is to use your 'home-grown' rocks, so that they are not being freighted long distances.

By far the cheapest method of buying rock if you need it in large quantities is to go direct to the quarry. You will pay the same amount of carriage whether it is for a ton or for ten tons, as it is charged per lorry load, so it is a good idea to split a load with a friend. Otherwise go to a garden centre, which does have the advantage that you can pick out the individual pieces you want, which you obviously cannot do in a quarry.

When you come to move the rocks around the garden into position console yourself with the thought that if Stonehenge and the Egyptian pyramids could be created with muscle power and a few simple tools, then you can surely construct a rockery. If you are not muscled like Hercules, then you can lever smaller stones into a wheelbarrow, wheel them to roughly the place that you want them, and roll them out. You can then use a combination of rolling and levering to place them where you want them. You can also drag surprisingly large stones around on empty compost bags.

The cheapest source of large rocks for garden features is your local quarry

Different methods for moving large rocks: top, smaller ones can be levered into a wheelbarrow; bottom, larger pieces can be moved on rollers made from household guttering downpipe

practice run with the rocks arranged on a lawn, drive or other open space is a good idea before committing yourself to digging in the rocks, starting from the ground level and building upwards. At least one third to half of each rock will need to be bedded into the ground to avoid potential for movement, slippage and accidents.

Your soil pockets can be customized for the plants you are using; an uncompromising 'desert' landscape, using hardy cacti and succulents, needs maximum drainage so mix half-and-half sharp sand or horticultural grit with your soil. Lush growers need less sharp drainage. You can also build in ready-camouflaged sites for dropping in half-hardy plants in their pots during the spring and summer to extend the range of plants.

You can move large rocks on a system of rollers, constructed from a length of plastic household guttering downpipe sawn into equal length pieces. Lever the first cylinder under the leading edge of the rock, then roll the rock over the remainder. You can push the rock all over the place – and steer it – like a little car, up and down gentle slopes and over gravel. As the rock moves forward keep adding the last roller from the back to the front. Alternatively, if this sounds too exhausting, you could always have a 'rockery barbecue', and swap the muscle power of your friends and family for a good feed afterwards. Once you have located or constructed your slope, position your rocks with a slight backward and downward slope, to give the outcrop illusion more credibility. This makes the structure safer because it is more stable, and as water will run backwards into the soil crevices, you can ensure that the plants will obtain sufficient moisture. A

Close up of soil pockets between the rocks

Planting up a stratified rockery with hardy cacti in a gritty soil mixture, for maximum drainage

You can make a boulder rockery on a completely flat site. This two-layer rockery, lined with permeable membrane, will look dramatic and be free-draining enough for most cacti

ii) BOULDER ROCKERIES

These are increasingly popular, because they are so bold and dramatic and can be used on a totally flat site. They depend on the use of water-smoothed boulders or quarried stones and again, the larger the better. A single huge boulder, or a group of large stones, looks very effective and their sculptural shapes can make as big an impact as a stratified rockery, with less time, effort and outlay. A permeable membrane liner for the base is highly recommended for future maintenance.

They also combine well with gravel and scree gardens, where the boulder rockery can fade into the surrounding gravel and stones by using progressively smaller, rocks, until you reach cobble, then pebble, size. A boulder-filled depression can meander through a gravelled area as a putative dried-up stream bed. Large boulders and rounded cobbles, with scrambling plants clambering over and between make a high impact display; these features also lend themselves to a dramatic and spiky planting, using cordylines, yuccas, hardy cacti and agaves etc. Depending on how macabre your tastes are, you can add a well-boiled (or bleached) sheep skull to add to the effect.

Boulder rockeries also combine well with water features and can be used as a visual link between ponds without the technical difficulties of actually constructing a flowing stream.

Boulder cheats

If you are not a purist, or the budget cannot be stretched adequately, you can use the recipe that was given in Chapter 7 for making streams and watercourse features to construct lightweight 'boulders' at a fraction of the price, using one part cement to two parts multi-purpose compost to three parts soft (builders') sand.

You will need an area of the garden, which you can dig out in a series of depressions, to act as moulds for your rocks. Line the moulds with polythene sheeting, and reinforce large or complex shapes with chicken wire. After the soil and cement mixture has set, carefully remove your 'rocks'. They are really easy to move around until they create an interesting arrangement and with time, the soil in the mixture encourages a very naturalistic growth of moss to give a weathered impression. To

The finished boulder rockery is planted up with an assortment of hardy cacti and succulents, which will relish the raised soil level and free root run

On the left, weathered mock rocks compared to a new mock rock on the right

speed this process you can either bury them for a time or paint them with a yoghurt mixture. Dilute a pot of unsweetened natural yoghurt with enough water to turn it into a thin emulsion, which you can paint onto rocks, troughs, statues etc. to encourage plant growth. Mock rocks best lend themselves to a rounded boulder shape as jagged edges are prone to cracking off.

iii) FLAT SLABS AND PAVEMENTS

Another smaller scale rockery is the pavement style, which involves the use of large flat slabs, e.g. slate, York stone etc., with interesting texture and riven surfaces. These can be laid in a shallow, overlapping rockery, with the same backward and downward slope, but this can be a small feature in an otherwise flat bed, lawn etc. A permeable membrane liner is a good idea as once invasive weeds or grasses get a foothold amongst the slabs it is nearly impossible to eradicate them unless you lift the slabs and start all over again.

Alternatively lay the rockery as a literal pavement, pathway or patio, or an unusual entrance-way to the house or garden. In this case the slabs need to be level and smooth to make a firm surface for walking on and they are laid with wide, compost-filled joints, ranging from 5–20cm (2–8in) square ready for planting up with tough, carpeting, hardy succulents.

iv) DRYSTONE WALLS AND RAISED BEDS

Walls without mortar make another wonderful medium for cacti and succulents, as, again, it gives them a dry, well-drained site with angled growth to throw off excess water. The maximum height should not exceed 0.6–1m (2–3ft) and the wall should consist of attractive stones laid layer upon layer, angled backward and downwards for security, so that any movement is back into the retaining soil and not down onto unsuspecting passers by. The rocks should run in alternating courses, so that each rock is laid across two supporting rocks underneath for safety. The soil acts as mortar, so should be well compressed into all the joints between the stones. Plants will grow happily in the joints and also along the top of the wall itself.

The same technique applies to the construction of an attractive raised bed. In this case, the walls are built so that they construct a rectangular surround to a bed consisting of about 25cm (10in) of soil, topped with as much again of a sharp soil/gravel mix, and topped with gravel and perhaps rocks and pebbles, with planting all around the sides and in the bed itself.

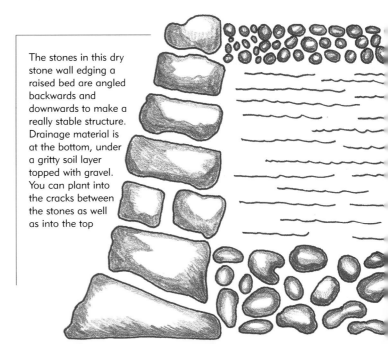

The stones in this dry stone wall edging a raised bed are angled backwards and downwards to make a really stable structure. Drainage material is at the bottom, under a gritty soil layer topped with gravel. You can plant into the cracks between the stones as well as into the top

An alternative raised bed involves using ready-made log roll, which can be used for edging paths etc. This consists of regularly sized cylinders of preservative-treated wood which is wired together in a flexible strip which can be rolled out in any shape you choose. It also makes an attractive rustic 'wall' for a bed.

Decide on the height of the bed as the roll comes in heights of either 15cm (6in) or 30cm (1ft). You can use the taller rolls for larger growing plants, while the smaller one makes a visually effective kerb for lower growing species.

Next choose your site, ideally well away from other features so that the bed has maximum impact. It can function as a divider between other garden features or as a stand-alone feature.

In the large bed illustrated, the roll was laid out on a gravelled area, and because this was already membrane lined, the gravel was simply moved away. In an area with soil, introduce a membrane layer to prevent the ingress of weeds.

Decide on the site of your bed and lay out the roll to shape. Remember that there is a right and a wrong way up. The wiring which holds the strip of logs together is fastened in two parallel lines, one of which is very close to the edge of the wood; this side faces down, otherwise unsightly wire lines will show above the soil when the bed is filled.

The roll is flexible so it can assume any shape you want. We chose an asymmetrical shape, so we wired the narrowest waisted part together by using strong wires fastened across the top and bottom of the bed. The bed was lined with a good layer of hard core, followed by a gravel layer and topped with a generous amount of gritty compost. After it was planted up, it was top dressed with a good layer of pea shingle.

You can add a second level, by laying a 15cm (6in) deep log roll in a similar, smaller shape on top of the first bed. These rolls also make attractive low-edged beds for smaller planting schemes.

Irregular rockery stones also make a fabulous raised bed. Use a variety of large, asymmetrical rocks, which are butted up together in a rough oval outline. Keep the inner profile between each rock in a 'v' shape because you will want your planting pockets to extend right up into the edges of the rocks. Again, use a good mix of hard core and gravelly soil to fill in the rough oval. You can keep this as a single layer bed, or you can use another layer of rocks to create a second, dramatic inner raised bed, with an elevated planting area.

Log roll beds are good for making asymmetrical shapes, like this one standing on permeable membrane

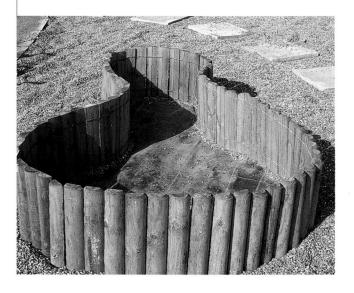

Wire the sides of the bed together to hold its shape. Line it with black polythene and cover the base with rough drainage material. Then add a good layer of gravel

Right: the gravel is then topped with a gritty soil mixture and finished off with a decorative gravel dressing.

Below: the completed bed is planted up, from l to r clockwise, with *Crassula pellucida* subsp. *marginalis*, *Echeveria* 'Afterglow', *Cereus jamacaru*, *Portulacaria afra*, *Euphorbia fasciculatus*, *Kleinia repens*, *Rochea coccinea*, *Opuntia subulata*, *Aloe davyana*, *Graptoveria* 'Hahinii', *Crassula volkensii*, *Sedum pachyphyllum*, *Echeveria* 'Reinelt', *Aeonium tabuliforme*, *Aloe wickensii*, *Portulacaria afra* 'Foliisvariegatus, *Aloe variegata*

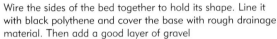

v) THE LOGGERY

In an area untroubled by honey fungus, old logs make wonderful subjects for planting up. This is an interesting and naturalistic effect, and makes a great conversation piece. The combination of the natural textures and colours of the wood with tiny colourful plants growing in the crevices is always very appealing.

You can use one log as a feature in a gravel bed, which would function as a miniature rockery in its own right. This can be planted with entirely tender subjects, then moved wholesale for the winter. In this case, you could try a themed log – with echeverias, say, crassulas, or with tiny cacti. You can use sempervivums as a totally weatherproof alternative.

To plant up the log, you will need to chisel out a series of depressions which can be treated as planting containers, filled with a compost mixture which is pushed well down into the crevices you have made. You will need to construct these at an angle, so that the plants sit in a pocket, sloping at about 45 degrees, into which they can fit securely. The plants are then pushed into position and watered in well to bed them in. As the roots grow, they will take a firm hold through into the surrounding wood and make a remarkably long-lasting and natural feature.

Alternatively you can stack your logs in a stepped series, almost as you would if you were using rocks, for a loggery on a larger scale. Again, aim at an integrated effect by lining the logs up in a regular stepped sequence. Bed each log firmly into the soil, again remembering the rule of downward and backwards for safety and moisture retention. You can use a dramatic specimen plant, like a large phormium as a spectacular backdrop, then plant the logs with a variety of creeping and trailing plants; echoing the spiky phormium leaves with the more compact shape of grasses, or the black *Ophiopogon planiscapus* 'Nigrescens'.

This kind of wooden rockery can also be repeated using wooden railway sleepers, or low woven fences of willow to retain each rockery step.

Once you have chosen your log, assemble your tools and lay a large sheet of black polythene to collect the chippings

A series of depressions is chiselled out, ready to be used as planting pockets

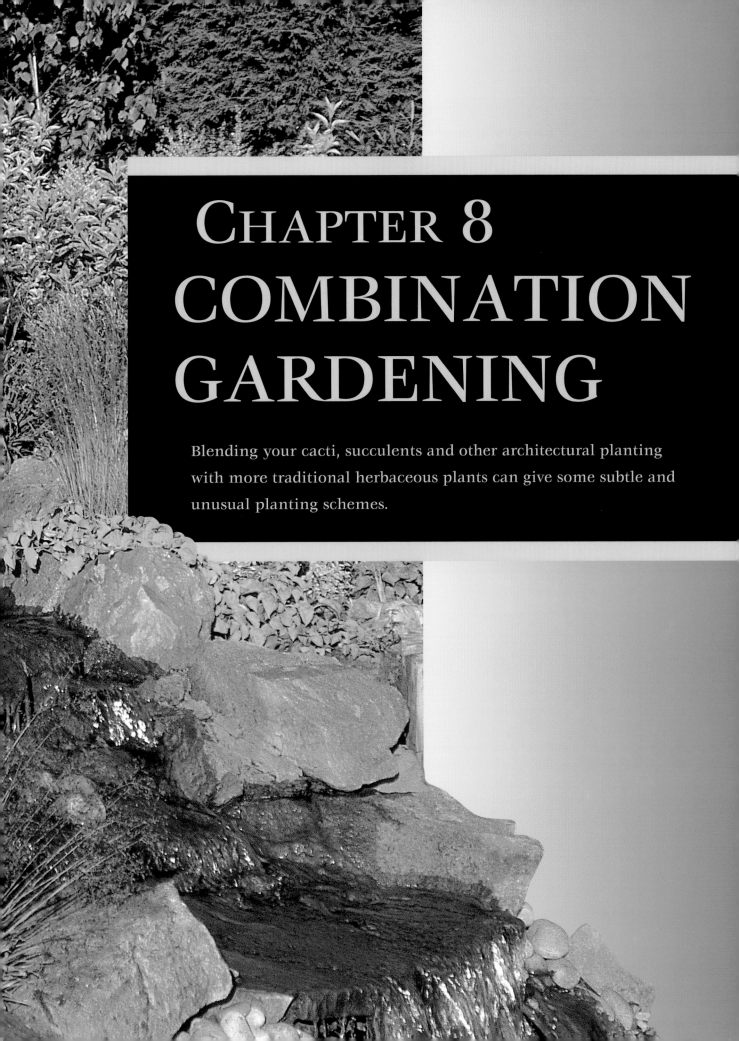

CHAPTER 8
COMBINATION GARDENING

Blending your cacti, succulents and other architectural planting
with more traditional herbaceous plants can give some subtle and
unusual planting schemes.

This urn contains a mixed planting with *Phormium* 'Evening Glow' as a bright centrepiece, softened by *Sedum spathulifolium*, and a trailing variegated ivy

APPLICATIONS

Combination gardening takes a different approach to what can be a radical and uncompromising style of gardening. Instead of using cacti and succulents plus some appropriate architecturals to shout their individuality these plants can, instead, actually be blended into a more conventional garden landscape, by adding unconventional touches more subtly. This is a popular approach, for a number of reasons.

The first is probably economy. Any total makeover is going to be expensive, and these exotic schemes are no different, particularly as a blank canvas needs instant height from expensive specimen plants, which could otherwise be bought in at an earlier and cheaper stage and allowed to mature *in situ*. People do not necessarily want to commit a huge slice of household income solely to gardening.

The second is time. Again, like cash, time is precious and usually in short supply. Most people's lives are already a delicate balancing act, and a wholesale total commitment to a massive garden scheme can strain more resources than the purely financial.

The third factor is one of sheer practicality. Often you already have a garden of which you are proud, or with which you are happy. Unless you are moving into a completely new property with a virgin garden, there are generally features that you want to keep. You may have acquired them ready-made by moving into a property with a mature garden, or you may have planned and planted them yourself. Gardens don't come quickly and it is more than most people can bear to slaughter their vision before or as it comes to maturity.

You may have spent money, time and dreams on a perfectly colour-schemed flower border *à la* Gertrude Jekyll or on achieving an immaculate lawn. You may have fallen in love with a bucolic daydream of a recreated Victorian cottage garden plot, or have gone for an ecologically sound mini-woodland area with an unfolding carpet of spring bulbs, followed by a purple blaze of bluebells and then cowslips to die for. Practical considerations may dictate that you need to provide a safe open space for your children's play area, or you want a vegetable garden to provide fresh produce straight from the garden to the table and free from pesticide residues.

In all of these cases, you may want to incorporate some of the plants and ideas that for their copious and attractive pea-like flowers which come in some attractive bi-colours, like yellow and bronze *C.* 'Firefly' and red and yellow *C.* 'Goldfinch'.

Lavandula (lavender) is a genus of evergreen shrubs, summer flowering with aromatic grey-green leaves and dense spikes of lavender to blue flowers. Smell the Med! Good for low hedging.

Rosmarinus officinalis (edible rosemary) is another aromatic choice, with small, dark green, glossy evergreen leaves and blue flowers. Growing up to 1m (3ft) or so tall, it also makes an interesting low hedge.

Santolina chamaecyparissus (cotton lavender), is a compact, hardy, rounded evergreen plant with lovely feathery silver foliage and bright yellow, button-like flowers in the summer. It reaches a height of 30cm (1ft) with a spread of 0.9m (35in). Prune hard in the spring to maintain compact growth. It likes light, well-drained soil.

Tamarix (tamerisk) is a graceful shrub, which has arching branches of narrow blue-green leaves and which bears large upright plumes of frothy, pink flowers in tall cloudy spires.

PERENNIALS
a) Fleshy leaves and sculptural forms
Gunnera manicata is a fabulous monster of an architectural plant, reaching 2m (6½ft) high and 2.2m (7ft) across, bearing enormous decorative frilled leaves almost like gigantic rhubarb leaves! It prefers a moist spot. It is hardy, but give it a sheltered spot to protect it from wind damage and also protect in winter,

e.g. by covering it with its own leaves anchored by soil on top.

Musa basjoo is the hardiest banana. This is a Japanese, suckering variety and you can expect several feet of growth in a year. It likes a light, sheltered position and it is a gross feeder so give it plenty of food and water. With protection (straw, bubble wrap or fleece) it can be left out for the winter, but it is probably easiest to treat is as a half-hardy subject.

b) Vivid colours and exotic flowers
We all love flowers and there are many flowering choices which associate very well with the architectural garden and its cacti and succulents. Look at gladioli, montbretia (crocosmia), lilies and irises.

Cannas are showy perennials which are grown for their wonderful flowers and for their ornamental foliage. They have lance-shaped leaves so they make a fabulous architectural impact, and they flower with dramatic spikes of flowers, reminiscent of iris or gladioli, borne in mid-summer to early autumn. They are half-hardy perennials grown from rhizomes and are good for use as striking summer bedding and for eye-catching and unusual containers.

Cordyline australis and a fuchsia make an attractive and unusual combination in this garden

Cannas make wonderful summer bedding, and they fit well into architectural planting schemes, with their tall foliage and spectacularly bright flowers

Cannas like a sunny position and rich moist soil. Lift and store the rhizomes in slightly damp peat or soil over the winter; they can be brought into growth in the spring under glass for early display, or set out when the danger of frost has passed. They can be divided in the spring. There are brown-leaved and green-leaved varieties, plus dwarf forms, so look out for the following amongst many others:

Canna green-leaf varieties:
'Brilliant', reaches 0.7m (27in) in height, red flowers
'Felix Regout', height 1m (3ft), yellow flowers
'Mrs Oklahoma', height 1m (3ft), pink flowers
'Orange Perfection', height 1m (3ft), orange flowers
'Salmon Pink', 0.75m (2½ft) high, salmon flowers

Canna brown-leaf varieties:
'Black Knight', 0.8m (32in) high, very dark red flowers
'Red King Humbert', 1.5m (5ft) high, scarlet flowers
'Tirol', 1m (3ft) high, pink flowers
'Wyoming', 1.5m (5ft) high, orange flowers

Canna dwarf varieties:
'Crimson Beauty', 0.45m (1½ft) high, dark red flowers and green leaves
'Golden Lucifer', 0.4m (16in) high, yellow speckled flower with green leaves
'Louise Cotton', 0.5m (20in) high, copper-orange flowers, brown leaves
'Lucifer', 0.4m (16in) high, red flowers with a yellow edge, green leaves
'Opera La Boheme', 0.4m (1½ft) high, pink flowesr, green leaves

Heucheras are actually desirable not for their flowers but for their fabulous coloured leaves, so I have sneaked them in regardless! There is a really good choice of heucheras with brown, red and purple leaves, including *Heuchera* 'Palace Purple', an evergreen hardy perennial, with heart-shaped deep purple leaves and delicate white flowers. See too 'Chocolate Ruffles', with brown leaves with a maroon underside and small white flowers; 'Helen Dillon' with its variegated cream speckled green leaves and red flowers; 'Persian Carpet' with red/silver leaves and 'Pewter Moon' and 'Pewter Veil' with brown-grey upper leaves and pink flowers. They associate well with all of the grey-leaved succulents and make a wonderful hanging basket choice (which needs a good deal of watering, however).

Kniphofia, the renowned red hot pokers, come in a variety of mixed hybrids as well as in the traditional red form. They are perennials with spiky green leaves and dramatic flowers which are available in shades of red, yellow, orange and cream, plus bi-colours.

Strelitzia reginae, the stunning bird of paradise, with its fabulous beak-like orange and blue flowers with red-edged bracts, is a marvellous summer feature, but it has to be treated as half hardy.

c) Good architectural and/or golden or grey-leaved forms
Achillea. These have ferny, filigree-like grey leaves and large flat flowers. Look for 'Coronation Gold' with its long succession of yellow flowers and *A. filipendulina* 'Cloth of Gold' with deep yellow flowers.

Allium (ornamental onions). Attractive globular flower heads on long stems above pointed leaves.

Angelica archangelica (edible angelica). An upright perennial, which can reach 2m (6½ft), with divided bright green leaves and heads of white and green flowers.

Aquilegia vulgaris 'William Guinness' is an excellent hardy perennial choice for the purple-black colour scheme; it has deep purple to nearly black flowers, with white sepals, reaching about 0.7m (27in) high. There is also *A. vulgaris* var. *stellata* 'Black Barlow' with black flowers, bi-coloured purple-black and white *A. vulgaris* var.

This oriental pot, containing a *Trachycarpus fortunei*, makes a good contrast placed alongside a mixed herbaceous border

flore-pleno 'Magpie' and a pure white hybrid *A. vulgaris* var. *stellata* 'Sunlight White'.

Artemesias are a whole group of sun-loving, low-growing herbaceous perennials with finely cut, cloudy-looking, silver foliage; look specially for evergreens *A. ludoviciana* 'Silver Queen' and *A. alba* 'Canescens'.

Cardoon (*Cynara cardunculus*), is a 2m (6½ft) high x 1m (3ft) spread perennial making large clumps with arching, pointed silver-grey leaves and carrying huge purple-blue thistle-like flower heads on top of long grey stems.

Centaureas come in a range of annuals and perennials with thistle-like flower heads. Look for *C. cyanus*, a fast-growing silver-leaved annual reaching 30cm (1ft). *C. dealbata* is a 1m (3ft) perennial with lilac flowers and divided leaves. See also robust perennial *C. macrocephala*, which also has deeply cut leaves, with yellow flower heads with papery bracts.

Aquilegia vulgaris var. *flore-pleno* 'Magpie' is an attractive bi-coloured flower which goes well in a purple and black colour scheme

Semi-succulent *Euphorbia characias* subsp. *wulfenii* makes an attractive, textured blue-green mass in the border, with unusual heads of yellow-green blooms

Echinops bannaticus, also known as blue globe and globe thistle. This is a vigorous hardy perennial with large, round, spiky pale blue flower heads in the summer on upright stems with prickly dark leaves. It likes sun and a poor, well-drained soil. Grows to 1–1.5m (3–5ft) in height with a 0.75m (2½ft) spread. *Echinops ritro*, another globe thistle, is a hardy perennial with prickly leaves and upright stems bearing round blue flowers in the summer. It likes full sun and tolerates any soil, and it reaches a height of 1.2m (4ft) with a spread of 0.75m (2½ft).

Eryngium alpinum, sea holly, an upright perennial with purple-blue cone-like flower heads in July/August growing to 1m (3ft) high. It likes sun and a well-drained position. *Eryngium planum*, this is a fabulous sea holly. The dark green leaves are nondescript, but this hardy, thistle-like plant more than earns its place in any garden by producing beautiful, intensely blue, flowering stems, reaching over 0.9m (35in) in height, topped with many heads of tiny blue flowers surrounded by spiky blue bracts. *Eryngium varifolium* is a wonderful, architectural addition. This is a hardy, rosette-forming, evergreen perennial with spiky, stiff leaves, which are green marbled with white, and bearing striking thistle-like blue-green flowers in late summer. It grows 0.45m (1½ft) high.

Euphorbias are good for flowers and foliage, but their sap irritates the skin so beware. They have fleshy leaves and interesting heads of lime green or yellow flowers. See particularly evergreen *E. myrsinites*, reaching 15cm (6in) high, with its blue-green trailing leaves and yellow-green flower heads carried from mid-spring to early summer. *E. amygdaloides* 'Purpurea' has bright red leaves and shoots in the spring, maturing to mahogany, with green-yellow flowers in mid- to late spring and reaching 30–40cm (12–15in) high. *Euphorbia characias* subsp. *wulfenii* has textured blue-green leaves and yellow-green flowers. See also sun- and warmth-loving *E. characias* 'Burrow Silver' which reaches a metre (3ft) high and has variegated green and white leaves and bright yellow flower spikes from early to late spring.

Helichrysum italicum subsp. *serotinum* is also known as the curry plant, for its unusual scent. It forms a compact evergreen dome of densely felted grey-green leaves and it has vivid yellow flowers; although frost hardy it hates overwatering.

Hostas. Look for gold and yellow variegated forms, like *H.* 'Golden Tiara', *H.* 'Gold Standard', *H. montana* 'Aureomarginata', *H. ventricosa* var. *aureomaculata*. Or white and green variegated forms like *H. undulata* var. *univittata*, *H. crispula* and *H. decorata*. A good dressing of gravel around the base of the plants will deter slugs.

Onopordum acanthium, or Scotch thistle, is a showy biennial with wonderful silver-grey foliage and purplish-pink flowers. It grows to 2m (6½ft) high.

Liatris spictata 'Floristan Violett' is a hardy perennial with clumps of grass-like foliage, reaching 1m (3ft) in height, and bearing tall stems of lilac flowers in late summer. It likes rich soil and sun.

Stachys has soft woolly grey leaves and spikes of pink flowers; 'Silver Carpet' is a non-flowering ground cover form.

Verbascum has grey basal rosettes of leaves and candelabra-like yellow flowers.

d) Mediterranean plants and shrubs
Here, look for the shrubs and herbaceous plants that are adapted to survive in drier areas; they have a natural affinity with the more succulent plants. You can choose a variety of grey and silver-leafed plants, plus aromatic scented herbs listed under shrubs, perennials and alpines.

In the summer you can add the aromatic citrus, like *Citrus aurantium* var. *myrtifolia* 'Chinotto', the miniature orange tree and *C. limon*, the miniature lemon tree for added Mediterranean scent and appearance. They will have to go indoors for the winter, though.

Look out, too, for *Olea europeae*, the olive tree, which is a slow-growing evergreen, with grey-green surfaced leaves with silvery undersides. This is hardy in a sheltered position and it likes full sun and a fertile soil.

Callistemon laevis or bottlebrush, are evergreen shrubs with narrow and pointed leaves, grown for their fabulous red flowers whose long stamens give them the bottle-brush appearance. This is hardy but give it a sheltered position, full sun and a rich soil.

Nerium oleander (oleander), is a lovely flowering evergreen upright shrub, with dark green leaves and clusters of red and white flowers. This is said to be frost tender. However, it grows on hundreds of miles of Spanish motorway central reservations in areas which are freezing cold in winter and boiling hot in summer, so it is probably worth a try out in the winter. Please be warned that all parts of the plant are very toxic.

This pretty pot is just waiting for a dramatic cordyline, phormium or agave to complete the centrepiece of this mixed planting

Grasses, like self-seeding annual *Briza maxima*, or quaking grass, and the perennial *Holcus mollis* 'Albovariegatus' combine very well with architectural plantings

e) Ornamental grasses
Another must-have for the combination garden. These are hardy, tolerant choices, with a subtle colour range. Wonderful for contrast in the mixed border or for architectural display in gravel beds or as striking container plants.

Arundinaria variegata is actually a dwarf bamboo, with narrow evergreen leaves striped with bold green and white. This is a slow-spreading form, reaching 0.75m (2½ft) high with an indefinite spread.

Agrostis canina 'Silver Needles' has shimmering, deciduous tufts of slender green and white foliage, with an eventual height of 25cm (10in) and a spread of 0.4m (16in). This is a fully hardy plant but you will need to cut back dead foliage in early spring before growth starts. It prefers a well drained but moist soil in sun or partial shade.

Carex morrowii 'Variegata' is a very attractive evergreen hardy perennial grass, forming a dense tuft of narrow green leaves with white striping. It reaches 30 x 30cm (1 x 1ft) and it enjoys a moist soil in sun or semi-shade. *Carex comans* 'Frosted Curls' has lovely, silvery-green arching leaves which curl at the tips. This is an evergreen, fully hardy sedge, forming a dense clump with a brown flower spike in early summer. It reaches 20cm (8in) high and 35cm (15in) spread, and it likes a moist and preferably acid soil and sun or light shade. *Carex secta* var. *tenuiculmis* has splendid long, arching dark bronze-brown grassy leaves from a central clump. It prefers moist soil in sun or partial shade, and it reaches a height and spread of 0.45m (1½ft). Cut back dead foliage before growth starts in the early spring.

Festuca glauca 'Golden Toupee' is an outstanding evergreen perennial, with dense golden foliage, reaching 25 x 25cm (10 x 10in) and thriving in dry conditions. *Festuca glauca*, or blue fescue, is one of the best of the blue-leafed grasses. This is a hardy, tuft-forming perennial with evergreen, thin and spiky foliage and a height and spread of 15cm (6in). *Festuca gautieri* grows into a striking hardy bright green mound. It likes a sunny position and it grows 20cm (8in) tall.

Holcus mollis 'Albovariegatus' is an attractive cultivar. This variegated, evergreen, creeping soft grass, striped white and green is a dwarf grower and very hardy. Planted in a mass it creates an almost white effect. With an eventual height of 30–45cm (1–1½ft) and an indefinite spread, it likes sun or partial shade.

Koeleria glauca is an unusual and very hardy evergreen perennial grass with attractive bluey-grey-green foliage, which is a useful contrast for many plants in the mixed border. It has a compact habit, reaching a height of 0.45m (1½ft) and a spread of 30cm (1ft).

Phalaris arundinacea var. *picta*, common name gardener's garters, is one of the most striking of the white and green striped grasses. It is a hardy herbaceous perennial with a spreading habit and insignificant flowers, and it reaches a height (in flower) of 1m (3ft) and has an indefinite spread.

f) Grass-like plants
Ophiopogon jaburan, the snake grass, is a hardy spiky evergreen, with dark green arching stems. Choose also *Ophiopogon planiscapus* 'Nigrescens', a big name for this fascinating hardy, evergreen. It is a spreading clump-forming perennial, grown for its distinctive grass-like black leaves and it bears lilac flowers and black fruits.

g) Climbers
For exotic flowers add marginally hardy bougainvillaea, like *B. glabra* 'Sanderiana', which is a vigorous and evergreen climber with dark green leaves and many bright purple flower-like bracts.

Passiflora caerulea, the blue passion flower, is another exotic hardy climber which needs support. It has dramatic white to pink tinged flowers, 7.5–10cm (3–4in) across, with purple, blue and white coronas, carried in the summer to early autumn. It likes full sun to slight shade and it is a wonderful subject for a wall or a fence. There are other less hardy passion flowers to choose from with a range of interesting flower shapes and colours including red flowering *Passiflora manicata* and *P. quadrangularis* which has almost tasselled centres.

Tropaeolum speciosum (flame creeeper or flame nasturtium) is a climber with lobed green leaves and bright red flowers. It likes shaded roots and can reach 3m (9ft) high.

h) Alpines and other small subjects
Ajuga reptans 'Braunherz' is a wonderful hardy alpine, with deep purple leaves and blue flowers.

Alyssum is a spreading evergreen with grey-green leaves and small yellow flowers.

Armeria maritima is a must for the dry garden. The sea pink or thrift is an evergreen, clumping fully hardy perennial. It has narrow grass-like dark green leaves and numerous, very pretty deep pink flowers in the summer. There is also a white-flowered variety.

Hardy *Corydalis flexuosa* has delicate fern-like foliage and pretty blue flowers.

Armeria maritima (thrift) in flower in a gravel bed with sedums amidst an interesting collection of half-buried old crockery

Annual *Mesembryanthemum criniflorum* (livingstone daisy) gives extra colour throughout the summer

Helianthemum (rock rose). These are evergreen spring- to autumn-flowering shrubs grown for their flowers, which come in a wide range of appetizing shades. They grow from 15–30cm (6in–1ft) high and are good rock garden choices.

Lampranthus roseus bears very pretty purple flowers, which are carried all summer on this low-growing mesembryanthemum. It has clumping grey-green leaves and it is hardy in mild areas (treat as half-hardy elsewhere). See also *L. spectabilis* with carmine pink flowers and pink-flowered *L. blandus.*

Lewisia cotyledon hybrids and *L.* 'Sunset' hybrids, evergreen, clumping perennials with rosettes of dark leaves. In early summer, they carry beautiful clusters of flowers in various shades of pink and white. They are hardy but appreciate good drainage.

Origanum (related to marjoram) is a spreading evergreen which comes in a range of gold-leaved and variegated forms.

Raoulia australis, creeping and mat-forming with minute grey leaves.

Thymus, the spreading thyme, comes as a variety of aromatic, spreading plants with tiny leaves in grey, gold, or variegated with small pink and purple summer flowers.

Sisyrinchium californicum Brachypus Group, also known as yellow grass, is a hardy alpine with sword-like foliage and star-shaped yellow flowers all summer. Reaches 15cm (6in) in height and enjoys a moist soil.

ANNUALS FOR EXTRA COLOUR

You can also scatter a seed packet full of annual, flowering *Mesembryanthemum criniflorum* (livingstone daisy) to add to your feast of flowers with a mass of colourful daisy-like blooms which open in the sunshine.

Pansies (*Viola × wittrockiana*) are also wonderful choices for rapid colour from seed, there are some excellent colourways including black and black and white choices. Look out for *V.* 'Black Star', 'Black Velvet', 'Blackjack' and 'Bowles Black'. There are also bi-colours like 'Silver Wings' and 'Rippling Waters' plus creams and whites to choose from. For bright colours there is a huge range to choose from, including 'Majestic Giants', with a wide colour range, and the single coloured 'Clear Crystals' series.

Portulaca margarita tropicals are sun-loving half-hardy annuals with fleshy, succulent leaves. They flower prolifically from early summer to mid-autumn with vivid, colourful flowers in a wide variety of colours. The plants are 23cm (9in) high with a 30cm (1ft) spread.

Annual climbers make a colourful backdrop to these schemes, like *Cobaea scandens*, the cup and saucer plant, with cup-shaped

The loose, drooping heads of *Borago officinalis*, the annual blue-flowered borage, make an attractive partner to the stiff-leaved *Phormium* 'Copper Beauty' in this informal planting scheme

neighbours. You will need to be vigilant to prevent the often more vigorous plants which are more adapted to the British climate from taking over. This has two functions; firstly to ensure the survival of all the plants you have selected, but also because these schemes can look very messy without clean lines.

Despite the watchwords being ruthlessness and vigilance, always look out for happy accidents. Some of the charm of gardening comes from the unexpected and unusual juxtapositions that nature can throw up at us, so don't waste them.

yellow-green flowers which turn to purple as they age. See, too, *Ipomoea hederacea* (morning glory) which has funnel-shaped convolvulus-like flowers in a wide range of colours from the traditional blue, to red, purple and pink. *Thunbergia alata*, black-eyed Susan, with its orange-yellow flowers with chocolate brown centres is another good choice.

HOW TO KEEP THEM LOOKING GOOD

As always, prevention is better than cure, so control is the secret here. If you have chosen isolation you need to maintain your areas of demarcation, e.g. by ensuring that a lawn surrounding an island bed is an immaculate frame, or that more vigorous alpines do not swallow up the tiny cacti and succulents in your rockery.

This is even more important in the mixed schemes. Often the cacti and succulents will grow happily but they cannot compete on equal terms with their native-born

Deep green rosetted *Aeonium arboreum* 'Zwartkop' glows against the orange backdrop of French marigolds (*Tagetes patula*)

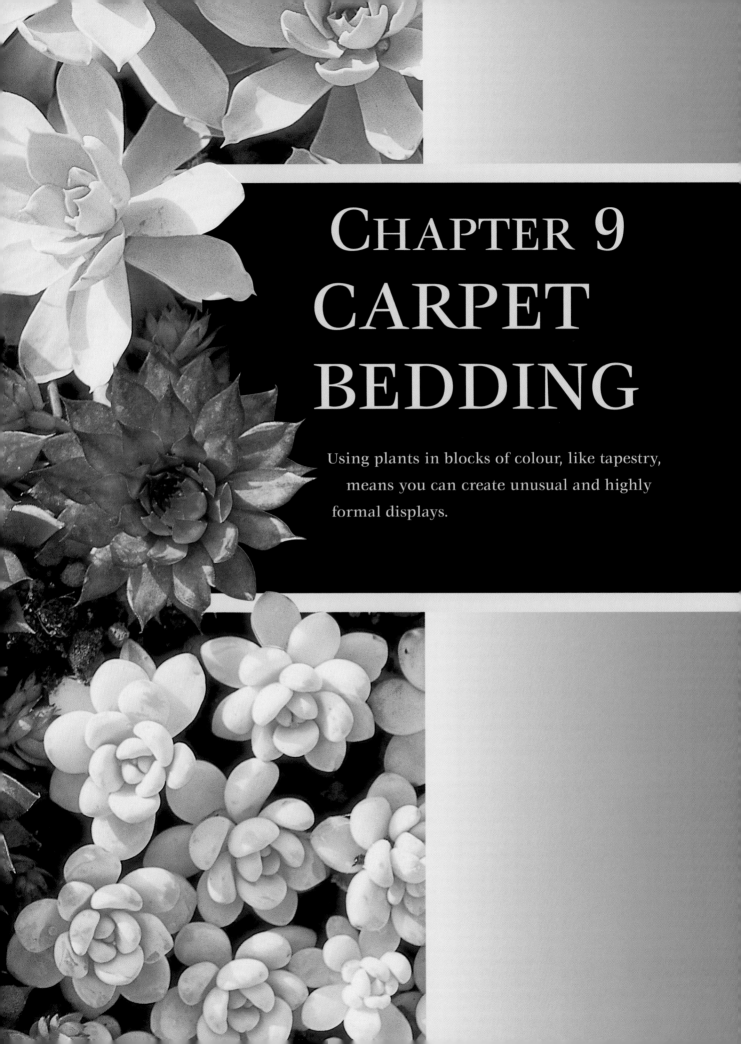

CHAPTER 9
CARPET BEDDING

Using plants in blocks of colour, like tapestry, means you can create unusual and highly formal displays.

APPLICATIONS

Carpet, or tapestry, bedding was much loved by the Victorians and Edwardians. It is also inextricably linked to the heyday of the British seaside and municipal parks, where it was used for coats of arms, floral clocks, initials, commemorative dates and signs of the 'Welcome to Skegness' variety. The basic form is a geometrical shape subdivided into many symmetrical areas, with low-growing and contrasting plants picking out the outlines and the infilling.

This is the most formal approach in this kind of gardening; it is the equivalent of topiary or the use of box hedging in knot gardens. As a result it is highly labour intensive and it requires large quantities of plants. 3m² (9ft²) requires about 500 plants and *pro rata* so it is not to be undertaken lightly. However, if you restrict your choice to succulent plants, it will require much less watering and maintenance than some of the other spreading varieties which are chosen, like tanacetum, kleinia, alternathera, ajuga etc.

It is also a really fun feature, which is very satisfying to plan and execute, either as small scale features with simple geometrical patterns, or in some huge scheme to celebrate something momentous – an important birthday, for example, or a birth, a special anniversary, or just a general celebration of your own family name.

SITING

The siting is crucial. This is a high impact project and for something which takes this much forward planning, construction time and maintenance the scheme needs to be well and truly visible, so consider insertion in a sloping bank, in a sunken area, in a position below a terrace, or under a window. As well as needing to be kept in immaculate condition itself, it also needs immaculate surroundings – a bowling green lawn, a paved surround, etc. to set if off and frame it.

This is an extremely formal approach to gardening, so it needs meticulous planning beforehand. You will need to make a scale drawing of the bed. Graph paper and coloured pencils will be helpful. A compass, set square and protractor for those without a fatal aversion to maths would also help.

Try out a variety of schemes before you make a final choice, but for your first attempt, keep it fairly simple. Select a geometrical figure for an outline shape, e.g. a rectangle, which you can then subdivide into diamonds, smaller rectangles, etc. You also need to decide whether your scheme is to be on one level or whether you want a three-dimensional effect with raised sections.

This is also in-your-face gardening. Go for strong contrast in colour and tone; the

A completed carpet bedding scheme, constructed in a mini walled bed. Top l, clockwise, *Echeveria dereceana, E. subsesillis, Sedum clavatum* and *E. derenbergii*, divided by a cross of deep red sempervivum cultivars

Before planting up, you must establish your centreline of plants, to ensure you have the symmetry that is essential to these schemes

The cross of sempervivums goes in first to give accurate planting guidelines for the rest of the plants

planting needs to be bold enough for the pattern to be clearly distinguishable; there's no place here for subtle harmonies.

CONSTRUCTION

When you have chosen your final scheme, size it up and draw it out – accurately – by pouring sand from a bottle or scraping the outlines with a sharp stick. You can use any straight-edged item for drawing straight lines, and a string attached to a cane will draw out circles, ovals etc.

If you have chosen a three-dimensional effect, you will need to build up some of the areas. Do this with care, because you do not want to spoil all your hard work with a landslide. Probably the easiest approach is to make a chicken wire outline, lined with membrane, almost like a giant hanging basket. This is, in effect, a raised bed with drainage material in the base covered with gritty topsoil. The sides of the raised structure are, of course, part of the planting scheme and can be planted up by pushing the root ball through the wire and membrane into the soil. You can go for

a halfway house by building up some sections with soil, following a gently curving profile, perhaps with some hard core as a foundation.

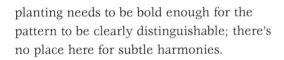

For a 3-D effect, you can make a simple, mounded, central section, following a gently curving profile, with drainage material as a foundation

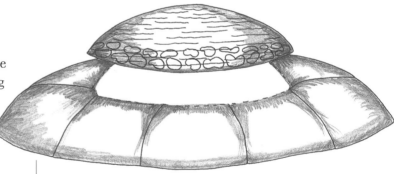

A more complex raised central area can be constructed out of chicken wire and lined with membrane. This is then filled with drainage material and soil and the plants are pushed through the membrane and wire to cover the sides

When you are planning a carpet bed on a small scale, you can arrange the plants on the surface, to make sure you have enough, and the effect is what you want. Here, contrasting sempervivums are used, with *Aloe aristata* as a centrepiece

For a small scheme, you can lay your plants on the surface before setting them to ensure regularity and that you don't run out of material. You need plenty of plants – although they will grow and intermingle, you don't want to start off too sparsely. For a large scheme you will need to draw out your design to scale and plant it up in sections with a pre-planned quantity of plants for each section. As a rule of thumb go for a 5cm (2in) spacing between the plants, and plant with care as you want this to look as meticulous as possible.

If the prospect of producing or buying the quantities of plants needed is too daunting, you can use a number of cheats. You can subdivide your infilled shapes with hard materials instead of more plants e.g. bricks, little paving stones, cobbles, etc. This also gives you a permanent framework for ringing the changes every year if you so wish.

The other possibility is to use box, an evergreen shrub, which is very good for edging like this. It can be propagated with semi-ripe cuttings in the summer. *Buxus sempervirens* 'Suffruticosa' is the best choice, and it can be kept trimmed to about 15cm (6in).

PLANTING SCHEMES

For a simple one-plant scheme, look at echeverias. These are also excellent choices for outlining the shapes before infilling with smaller plants.

GREY AND BLUE-GREY
Echeveria albicans, powdery grey-blue leaves, forming an attractive rosette
Echeveria amoena, small clustering blue-grey
Echeveria 'Blue Surprise', grey leaves with cream edges; rosette form
Echeveria 'Curly Locks', curly blue-grey rosettes, choice
Echeveria dereceana, pointed grey or grey-brown leaves with orange and yellow flowers
Echeveria elegans, branching species with intense grey bloom

After you have checked the scheme, and made any alterations, you can then bed the plants in. This bed is made in a log roll, which is 2.5m (8ft) long and 15cm (6in) high, and the picture was taken one month after initial planting

Echeveria glauca, grey-bloomed leaves in large rosettes, clustering, with rose pink flowers
Echeveria lindsayana, striking rosettes of pointed blue-grey leaves, tipped red, yellow flowers
Echeveria 'Lavender Hill', leaves have blue-grey inner surfaces which change to purple at the tips
Echeveria lutea, narrow variegated leaves, blue-grey and cream
Echeveria peacockii, rosettes of long tapering blue-white leaves; intense red flowers
Echeveria pulvinata 'Frosty', one of the most striking echeverias with beautiful grey leaves with white hairs; yellow flowers
Echeveria pilosa × harmsii, very attractive, downy succulent leaves, grey-green with deep red flushing when grown in sun, orange flowers
Echeveria subsessilis, rosettes of blue-grey leaves with red edges
Echeveria 'Sugard', grey felty leaves, bright orange flowers
Echeveria 'Van Keppel', stout triangular grey leaves forming a rosette, yellow flowers
Graptoveria 'Fanfare', rosettes of long narrow leaves with a blue-grey bloom, yellow flowers

RED, PURPLE AND LILAC
Echeveria 'Black Prince', like all the dark echeverias this is a highly prized 'catch'. Red-maroon to almost black leaves
Echeveria carnicolor, forms clumps of pink-lilac leaves
Echeveria 'Lavender Girl', rosettes of grey leaves with a lovely purple tinge
Echeveria 'Metallica' *cristate,* large growing, masses of tapering bronze-purple leaves
Echeveria 'Mexican Firecracker', colourful rosettes of 'felt'-covered leaves, brown-red below and green above
Echeveria 'Perle von Nurnberg', amazing purple-leaved hybrid

The tightly packed heads of *Echeveria gibbiflora* lend themselves to massed planting in blocks of colour

The pots of *Echeveria secunda* pictured here are in flower. However, unless you want a looser effect, it is best to take the buds off, to maintain your chosen colours and shapes

Graptoveria 'Albert Baynes', olive green and purple leaves, large growing

Graptoveria 'Mrs Richards', rosettes of maroon and grey leaves
Graptoveria 'Spring Morning', rosettes of leaves with a purple-grey bloom
Graptoveria 'Opalina', thick oval leaves covered in a red-grey bloom and arranged in a rosette
Pacheveria (Echeveria × Pachyphytum) scheideckeri 'Chimera', blue-grey rosettes

SHADES OF GREEN

Echeveria affinis, impressive dark olive green rosettes, almost black

Echeveria agavoides var. *prolifera,* rosettes of thick, light apple green, brown-tipped leaves forming large clumps

Echeveria 'Bouquet', narrow bright green pointed leaves with red edges

Echeveria mucronata, vigorous growing, pale green leaves

Echeveria multicaulis, branching stems bearing rosettes of dark green leaves with prominent red margins

Echeveria nodulosa, a real gem; dark green leaves with maroon veins

Echeveria 'Painted Frills', rosettes of wavy red, brown and olive green leaves

Echeveria 'Reinelt', apple green tapering leaves with red tips and edges

Echeveria 'Ron Evans', small clustering green rosettes with a red tip to each leaf

Echeveria setosa, a very unusual plant and one of the best echeverias. Green-grey leaves covered with dense white hairs

Graptoveria 'Titubans', elongating rosettes of light green leaves with grey-blue bloom

Kleinia repens, which is a beautiful blue-leaved species

For in-filling choose from a wide range of mat-forming sedums like:

GREY, SILVER, WHITE FOLIAGE

Sedum × *amecamecanum,* with scrambling or trailing stems covered in silver and green rounded leaves

Sedum cauticola 'Lidakense', tiny, grey-green succulent leaves

Sedum dasyphyllum, a low-growing, compact plant only 4cm (1½in) high, with a mass of grey foliage

Sedum dasyphyllum 'Lloyd Praeger', pale green early in the season, but later becoming grey

Sedum ewersii 'Nanum', a trailing perennial with blue-grey leaves and red flowers

Sedum hispanicum, mat-forming grey-green plants covered in miniature cylindrical leaves

Sedum pluricaule, a spreading plant, with small grey-green leaves

Sedum spathulifolium 'Cape Blanco' with flat rosettes of fleshy, silvery leaves

DARK BROWN, PURPLES AND BLACK

Sedum album f. *murale,* this is brown, bronze or purple

Sedum gypsicola, wine red leaves

Sedum spathulifolium var. *purpureum,* which has flat rosettes of fleshy grey and purple leaves.

REDS AND PINKS

Sedum album 'Coral Carpet', small rounded or cylindrical leaves, green, red and maroon

Sedum oreganum subsp. *tenue,* cherry red

Sedum × *rubrotinctum,* cherry red in the sun

Sedum spathulifolium 'William Pascoe', purple-red leaves

Sedum spurium var. *variegatum* (syn. *Sedum spurium* 'Tricolor'), a pretty variegated carpeting succulent, with green leaves, edged with white and flushed red in the sun

Sedum ellacombianum in flower in July. This is a good carpet bedder for large areas

Sempervivums can be used on their own to create carpet bedding which contrasts in colour and in form

SHADES OF GREEN

Sedum acre 'Yellow Queen', an evergreen, mat-forming perennial which has dense spreading shoots, clothed in tiny, fleshy, pale green leaves, variegated yellow

Sedum album var. *micranthum* subsp. *chloroticum* which has small, succulent bright yellow-green leaves

Sedum ellacombianum, with toothed green leaves

Sedum hispanicum var. *minus,* lovely blue-green leaves

Sedum makinoi 'Variegatum', green with cream and yellow variegation, flushed pink in full sun; half-hardy

Sedum middendorffianum, mat-forming with green-brown leaves

Sedum pachyclados, mound-forming species with dark green leaves

Other low-growing and spreading plants:

Aptenia cordifolia 'Variegata', freelybranching leafy succulent

Crassula alba, rosette-forming with pointed, fleshy leaves with finely serrated edges

Sempervivums:

GREY/WHITE

Sempervivum arachnoideum, small green rosettes with a fine 'cobweb' of hairs joining the leaf tips, giving a grey appearance

Sempervivum 'Congo', grey and maroon with 'felty' leaves

Sempervivum 'Grapetone', greyish green centre, lavender base

Sempervivum 'King George', compact green rosettes with white webbing at the edges of the leaves

Sempervivum 'Silver Jubilee', small, grey-green, with a 'cobwebby' appearance

Sempervivum 'State Fair', grey-green leaves

SHADES OF GREEN

Sempervivum funckii, bright yellow-green in spring, with light 'cobwebbing'

Sempervivum giuseppii, green, slightly hairy

Sempervivum 'Limelight', startlingly bright lime green

Jovibarba heuffelii 'Jade', light green

Jovibarba hirta subsp. *borealis,* tight packed, small yellow-green

Jovibarba sobolifera 'Green Globe', small, very bright green

Jovibarba sobolifera 'August Cream', very small, pale yellow-green

DARK RED SHADES

Sempervivum 'Dark Beauty', large, very dark red

Sempervivum 'Noir', very deep red

Sempervivum 'Prairie Sunset', large, warm orange-red

Sempervivum 'Purdy's', 'felty' maroon leaves

Sempervivum 'Purple Beauty', maroon-grey

Sempervivum 'Purple King', purple-red

Sempervivum 'Red Shadows', very deep red base with lighter tips

Sempervivum 'Rotkopf', red

This planting of *Echeveria secunda* is very effective, in this case surrounding the green spikes of *Ophiopogon jaburan* as a centrepiece

PINK SHADES

Sempervivum 'Caramel', delicious warm caramel colour – almost appetizing!

Sempervivum 'Gray Dawn', pink, greyish centre

Sempervivum 'Peach Blossom', warm peachy pink with green flushing

Sempervivum 'Pink Puff', small pink rosettes

Sempervivum 'Rose Splendour', deep pink

Sempervivum 'Spring Mist', small pink rosettes

Sempervivum 'Strawberry Fields', bright strawberry pink

BI-COLOURED

Sempervivum 'Blood Tip', leaves tipped red

Sempervivum 'Bronze Pastel', small bronze-pink

Sempervivum cantabricum, olive green, purple-tipped

Sempervivum 'Icicle', frosted green centre, pink outer

Sempervivum 'Jewel Case', pink with green centre

Sempervivum 'Night Raven', large maroon base with green tips

Sempervivum 'Nigrum', light green base with deep, blood red tips

Sempervivum 'Painted Lady', pink edged with yellow-green base

Sempervivum 'Pink Pearl', pale green-grey, tipped maroon

Sempervivum 'Red Flush', maroon-brown and olive green leaves

Sempervivum 'Rubrum Ash', red and grey rosettes

Sempervivum 'Sir William Lawrence', green with bright maroon-red tips to the leaves

Sempervivum 'Smokey Jet', outer deep pink; inner green

Sempervivum 'Stuffed Olive', very bright green centre, pink outer

Sempervivum 'Video', maroon and grey-green

Jovibarba heuffelii 'Apache', green base with purple/maroon tips

Jovibarba heuffelii 'Fandango', large, lime green base, tipped bright red from halfway up

Jovibarba heuffelii 'Greenstone', green centre and red tips

Jovibarba heuffelii 'Orion', very dark maroon with the outer edges tipped bright green

Jovibarba heuffelii 'Suntan', very contrasty; red tipped green

Jovibarba hirta 'Emerald Spring', small, very bright green tipped with maroon

Jovibarba hirta 'Inferno', very dark red with green at the very base

HOW TO KEEP THEM LOOKING GOOD

ACCENT PLANTS FOR THE CENTREPIECE
FEATURES OF A BED
*Aeonium tabuliforme, A. arboreum, A.
arboreum* 'Zwartkop'
Agave americana 'Variegata' plus other large
agaves, *Aloe aristata,* cordyline, phormium

It is essential to fill the beds because the aim
is to have total ground cover as quickly as
possible. On grounds of economy, therefore,
you may want to start propagating the plants
the previous year to ensure you have
sufficient quantities. These ground-covering
plants are all easy to propagate by taking off
segments, drying them out for a couple of
weeks, then setting them into slightly damp,
gritty compost.

A formal scheme like this needs to be
immaculate, so keep it weed-free.

Keep clipping the plants back if they threaten
to grow into one another and muddy your
outlines. Keep the clipping as precise as you
can to preserve the demarcation lines
between your blocks of pattern. You may find
that secateurs or even scissors give you the
most control in tight spaces, though you can
use shears on larger areas (smaller-bladed
ladies' models are ideal). Take away any cut
material, as nothing looks worse than
decaying plant material. Debud any plants
that attempt to flower, as foliage effects give
by far the cleanest lines. You do not want
these plants to flower and spoil the solid
blocks of colour. Keep some spares back to
infill if you have any casualties.

And if you really get the bug, start planning
ahead for next year's even grander scheme (a
clock or your coat of arms?) by propagating
the plants you will need in plenty of time.

A large-scale succulent carpet bedding scheme at
Waddesdon Manor near Aylesbury, southeast England,
featuring an abstract landscape created by artist John
Hubbard. The scheme was worked out from Hubbard's
original watercolour painting and preplanted on carpet tiles
at Kernock Park Plants in Cornwall using a computerized
system called InstaPlant (see Further Information)

CHAPTER 10
PLANT DIRECTORY

The 165 plants featured are divided into three sections for easy reference – fully hardy, hardy in milder areas and half hardy. There is at least one close up photograph of every plant listed, plus useful information on size and a full description of its characteristics to inspire you and help in your selection.

FULLY HARDY

*Aloe
aristata*

Size: 8cm (3in) high, 12cm (4in) across

Succulent, hardy in a well-drained rockery. Propagate from offsets. Forms dense groups of up to 12 stemless rosettes of dark green, narrow leaves with very soft spines. Branching flower stems up to 0.6m (2ft) tall bearing 20 or more red or pinkish flowers, carried in late spring in Europe.

*Armeria
maritima* (thrift)

Size: reaches 10cm (4in) high with a spread of 15cm (6in)

Hardy perennial. This plant is not a succulent but it is a must for the 'dry' garden; the sea pink or thrift is an evergreen, clumping fully hardy perennial, with narrow grass-like dark green leaves and numerous, very pretty deep pink or white flowers in the summer.

*Carex
oshimensis* 'Evergold'

Size: reaches 20cm (8in) height and spread

Hardy waterside grass. A bright yellow-striped and dense-growing sedge, with narrow, evergreen leaves, showy all year. It enjoys a sunny spot in moist soil.

*Carex
secta* var. *tenuiculmis*

Size: height and spread 0.4m (1½ft)

Hardy waterside grass. A splendid sedge with long, arching dark bronze-brown grassy leaves from a central clump. It prefers moist soil in sun or partial shade. Cut back dead foliage before growth starts in the early spring.

Size: reaches 30cm (1ft) high and 0.4m (1½ft) across

Hardy waterside grass. This is a pretty semi-evergreen perennial with heavily variegated, rigid, white-striped leaves. Like all the sedges, it likes a moist soil.

Carex 'Silver Sceptre'

Size: 1.5m (5ft) height and spread

Hardy palm. Slow growing and shapely, with stiff fan-shaped leaves, 0.6–1m (2–3ft) across and clumping trunks. An evergreen, it is very cold tolerant, down to as low as ⁻10C (14F). Also known as the European or Mediterranean fan palm.

Chamaerops humilis (dwarf fan palm)

CORDYLINES

The New Zealand lily palm; also known as the Cornish or Torquay palm. Very dramatic, architectural 'surrogate' palms. Sword-like leaves surrounding a woody stem; as this grows the leaves die off and can then be stripped back to reveal an attractive trunk. These are hardy in almost all circumstances; at worst they are cut down in a severe winter, when they resprout vigorously in the spring, producing a multi-headed plant which can be divided when the stems become woody. Alternatively they can be treated as a dramatic potted subject for half-hardy display in the warmer months, and moved into a conservatory for the winter.

Size: 15m (50ft) tall eventually, with a 5m (16ft) spread

Evergreen with green leaves and panicles of small white flowers in the summer. It makes an attractive, small tree for many years.

Cordyline australis

FULLY HARDY

Cordyline banksii

Size: 15m (50ft) tall eventually, with a 5m (16ft) spread

Another green-leaved cordyline, vigorous and upright growing, with rather longer leaves than *C. australis*, with a softly drooping habit.

Cordyline 'Coffee Cream'

Size: 15m (50ft) tall eventually, with a 5m (16ft) spread

This colourful evergreen has olive brown leaves with a yellowish mid-stripe. Cultivars like this are a little less vigorous than *C. australis*.

Cordyline 'Pink Stripe'

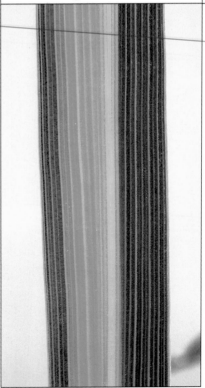

Size: 15m (50ft) tall eventually, with a 5m (16ft) spread

A very colourful cultivar, with dazzling striped leaves. The cultivars are a little less vigorous than *C. australis*.

Size: 15m (50ft) tall eventually, with a 5m (16ft) spread

An exciting deep red-brown variety, which makes a good contrast. The cultivars are a little less vigorous than *C. australis*.

Cordyline 'Purple Tower'

Size: up to 2.5m (8ft) tall with 1.2m (4ft) spread

Hardy grass. A wonderful specimen plant, this is an evergreen perennial, with narrow leaves, 1.5m (5ft) long, which arch dramatically yet gracefully outwards from the plant. Tall plumes of the flower panicles appear late summer, reaching up to 60cm (2ft).

Cortaderia selloana (pampas grass)

Size: up to 0.6m (2ft) high and 0.4m (1½ft) across

Succulent. Grows into an attractive miniature tree. Good in rockeries, by ponds or potted up as a 'bonsai' specimen. Likes full sun, when it grows as a compact shrub. It has narrow, dark green leaves and lots of pink or white flowers, produced in summer. Very frost resistant.

Crassula sarcocaulis

FULLY HARDY

Dicksonia antarctica
(tree fern)

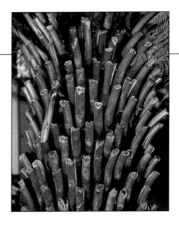

Size: ultimately 10m (30ft) high, 4m (12ft) spread, but very slow growing. Fronds 1m (3ft) or more long.

A primitive, evergreen, tree-like fern that resembles a palm. The stout trunks are covered with brown fibres and crowned with arching, much-divided, palm-like fronds. Prefers some shade, but will grow in full sun if watered. Loses leaves in winter.

Eryngium planum (sea holly)

Size: over 1.5m (5ft) high

Thistle-like perennial, though leaves die in autumn to regrow in spring. Produces beautiful, intensely blue stems, topped with many heads of tiny blue flowers, surrounded by showy, spiky, blue bracts, which can be dried for winter decoration. Flowers for several weeks from early August onwards.

Hakenochloa macra 'Aureola'

Size: reaches 0.45m (1½ft) high with a 0.6m (2ft) spread

Hardy grass. This makes a fabulous container subject or specimen plant, with its outstanding bright yellow-striped, arching leaves with lots of long-lasting contrasting red-brown flowers produced from the autumn onwards.

Juncus filiformis 'Spiralis'
(corkscrew rush)

Size: grows 20cm (8in) tall with a 30cm (1ft) spread

Hardy waterside grass. A fabulous plant, which is great fun for a wet spot by the pond, along with the sedges. It has evergreen tufts of green, contorted, twisting leafless stems, good-looking all year. Cut dead foliage down in the spring.

Size: height and spread vary from 1–1.5m (3–5ft) to 0.45–0.6m (1½–2ft)

Hardy perennial, related to the succulent African aloes, but not a succulent itself, though it does relish full sun. Propagate by division. Spiky green leaves, usually evergreen, and dramatic flowers, usually scarlet-orange, but can be white, cream and yellow through to orange.

Kniphofia
(red hot poker)

Size: 6 x 6m (20 x 20ft)

Hardy shrub. An evergreen, upright shrub with dark green, glossy, spiny-edged leaves and sweet-smelling flowers, carried from the early autumn to the early spring.

Mahonia
× *media* 'Charity'

Size: 2.5cm (1in) or so high with an indefinite spread

This carpeting succulent has fleshy bright green leaves which die back in winter but reappear every spring to clothe pond edges, rockery sites, etc. It carries abundant, beautiful bright yellow daisy-like flowers making a dazzling carpet in the spring.

Mesembryanthemum
'Basutoland'

Size: 23cm (9in) tall and 30cm (1ft) spread

A fascinating evergreen perennial, spreading and clump-forming, grown for its distinctive grass-like black leaves; it has lilac flowers and black fruit.

Ophiopogon
planiscapus 'Nigrescens'

FULLY HARDY

Phalaris arundinacea var. *picta* (gardener's garters)

Size: height (in flower) of 1m (3ft) and an indefinite spread

This evergreen grass is one of the most striking of the white and green striped grasses; it needs watching because it spreads readily. It has insignificant flowers.

PHORMIUMS

New Zealand flaxes, hardy, evergreen perennials, grown for their bold, sword-shaped leaves; architectural plants ideal for patios, tubs and interesting garden arrangements. Large-growing varieties make huge architectural subjects in time; dwarf forms are ideal for containers. Clumps can be divided.

Phormium 'Bronze Baby'

Size: grows up to 0.45m (1½ft) high and 0.6m (2ft) across

A strong-growing, evergreen, upright perennial with tufts of bold, stiff-pointed wine red leaves.

Phormium 'Rainbow (Maori) Maiden'

Size: reaches 0.75 x 0.75m (2½ x 2½ft)

Very showy perennial, with delicate weeping leaves in rich, rosy salmon pink to coral red, banded with bronze margins. Makes a wonderful specimen plant or a container plant. (Shown with *Yucca gloriosa* 'Variegata')

Size: reaching up to 2m (6½ft) high with a 2m (6½ft) or so spread

Hardy perennial. One of the biggest phormiums. A strong erect growing cultivar, with pale bronze leaves with a mainly red mid-stripe. New foliage is very pink. Large plants can be divided, so you have a chance of creating an unusual evergreen 'hedge'.

Phormium **'Sundowner'**

Size: 1 x 1m (3 x 3ft)

Hardy perennial. This vigorous phormium has green leaves, developing strong pale yellow variegation after the first few centimetres of growth. Yellow flowers and long black seed pods. The weeping form makes it a particularly effective specimen plant and a good container choice.

Phormium **'Yellow Wave'**

BAMBOOS

These are hardy exotic plants, perfect for fleshing out the architectural garden. They like a moist soil, so if you grow them in pots they will need plenty of water; they will put on a lot of growth each spring and summer. You can use them to make a delicate screen for the garden or as individual specimens in the garden or in containers.

Size: reaching 0.45m (15ft) in height

This is the most dramatic and desirable of the bamboos; the jet black stems develop when the plant is still quite young. Full sun brings out the best colour. Non-invasive, reaching maximum height with moist, rich soil conditions. Wonderful container subject or ideal specimen plant.

Phyllostachys nigra (black bamboo)

FULLY HARDY

Pleioblastus viridistriatus

Size: 1–1.5 m (3–5ft) high with an indefinite spread

This bamboo is a slow-growing evergreen, with a compact spreading habit. It has green and yellow variegated leaves on thin upright canes. It is good for mixed planting but it needs shade. Hardy to -23˚C (-9˚F).

Puya chilensis

Size: height and spread to 2m x 2m (6½ x 6½ft)

Hardy bromeliad. This is an upright evergreen with short, woody stems, crowned by a dense rosette of long, tapering, arching grey-green leaves. It is ferociously stiff and spiny. Tubular, metallic yellow flowers, carried in panicles, in the summer.

Raoulia australis (vegetable sheep)

Size: 1cm (½in) tall with 1m (3ft) spread

This is an evergreen, creeping and mat-forming perennial with minute, succulent grey leaves and tiny yellow flower heads in the summer. Good for rockeries, pond edges and to creep in the gaps in paving stones. It competes with other plants, growing over them.

Saxifraga 'Southside Seedling'

Size: 30 x 30cm (1 x 1ft)

Hardy perennial. This evergreen encrusted saxifrage has large rosettes of leaves, bearing striking red and white flowers.

Size: less than 2.5cm (1in) high and spreading up to 1m (3ft)

Another antipodean 'moss' or 'mat' plant, like *Raoulia australis*. A bright green carpeting perennial, with tiny, hard leaves forming a very tight mat. Inconspicuous flowers. Good for pond edging, between paving stones, dry stone walls etc., and 'clothing' features.

Scleranthus biflorus
(Australian astroturf)

Size: 2.5–5cm (1–2in) high with indefinite spread

This succulent, evergreen, mat-forming perennial has dense spreading shoots, clothed in tiny, fleshy, pale green leaves, variegated yellow; plus abundant small yellow flowers. Ideal for carpet bedding, pond edging etc.

*Sedum
acre* 'Yellow Queen'

Size: 5cm (2in) tall with an indefinite spread

A well-known, succulent perennial. Very vigorous and quite variable depending on whether it's grown in a drought-ridden position on a wall or more lushly in the ground. Leaves are small and blunt-ended, ranging from red to brown in dry conditions through to green.

*Sedum
album*

Size: 5cm (2in) tall with an indefinite spread

Hardy succulent perennial. This colourful cultivar has small rounded or cylindrical leaves, bright red and maroon in the sun. Mat-forming, so good for carpet bedding. Small white flowers.

Sedum album f. *murale*
'Coral Carpet'

FULLY HARDY

Sedum ellacombianum

Size: 4cm (1½in) high with an indefinite spread

Hardy succulent perennial. Bright green with toothed leaves and yellow flowers; a good carpeting subject for rockeries, pond edges, carpet bedding etc.

Sedum middendorffianum

Size: variable height from 4cm (1½in) with an indefinite spread

Hardy succulent perennial. This is another mat-forming species, with green-brown leaves and striking yellow-orange spiky flowers.

Sedum pachyclados

Size: from 4cm (1½in) high with an indefinite spread

Hardy succulent perennial. This a fabulous, creeping, mound-forming species with evergreen blue-green rosettes and masses of white or pinkish flowers.

Sedum spathulifolium var. *purpureum*

Size: 4cm (1½in) high with an indefinite spread

Hardy succulent perennial. With its flat rosettes of fleshy grey and purple leaves, this is an unusual and contrasting colour choice for carpet bedding. Clusters of small yellow flowers.

Size: from 4cm (1½in) high with an indefinite spread

Hardy succulent perennial. This is another sedum perfect for dramatic carpet bedding. Flat rosettes of fleshy, silvery leaves give another useful colour contrast; clusters of small yellow flowers.

Sedum spathulifolium **'Cape Blanco'**

Size: height and spread 45cm (18in)

Clumping hardy deciduous perennials, grown for their colourful flowers, As well as 'Brilliant' look for mauve/lilac 'Carmen' and white 'Iceberg'

Sedum spectabile **'Brilliant' (ice plant)**

SEMPERVIVUMS

House leeks, grow in symmetrical rosettes of fleshy leaves, forming hardy ground-hugging mats suitable for rock gardens, screes, walls, banks, container gardens and alpine houses. Star-shaped flowers; the rosettes die after flowering but are replaced by numerous offsets.

Size: 5–12cm tall (2–5in); 2.5–4cm (1–1½in) diameter rosettes, with a spread of 10cm (4in) upwards

Hardy succulent perennial. Evergreen, vigorous and mat-forming, with numerous small green rosettes with a fine 'cobweb' of white hairs joining the leaf tips. Ideal for rockeries, containers, paving, walls etc.

Sempervivum arachnoideum **(cobweb houseleek)**

FULLY HARDY

Sempervivum 'Caramel'

Size: 5–12cm tall (2–5in); spread 10cm (4in) upwards

Hardy succulent perennial. Like the species, this is evergreen, vigorous and mat-forming, but it is a delicious warm caramel colour – almost appetizing!

Sempervivum cultivar

Size: 5–12cm tall (2–5in); spread 10cm (4in) upwards

Hardy succulent perennial. A good deal of plant breeding has taken place and you will find numerous colourful cultivars, like this maroon one.

Sempervivum *calcareum*

Size: 5–12cm tall (2–5in); rosettes 6cm (2½in) in diameter, spread 10cm (4in) upwards

Hardy succulent perennial. This is an attractive species with grey-green leaves with purple tips and pink flowers.

Sempervivum cultivar

Size: 5–12cm tall (2–5in); spread 10cm (4in) upwards

Hardy succulent perennial. This is another evergreen, vigorous and mat-forming cultivar, in shades of purple and olive green.

Size: 5–12cm tall (2–5in); rosettes 2.5cm (1in) in diameter upwards and a spread of 10cm (4in) upwards

Hardy succulent perennial. A very variable species, with shades of green and brown with or without contrasting tips.

Sempervivum tectorum

Size: height up to 12m (40ft) eventually

This palm has stiff fan-like leaves and a slim, solitary trunk. The plants are attractive at all stages, making pretty shrubs when small with their regular circle of leaves, and covetable subjects for many years as they develop in height. They are very cold tolerant.

Trachycarpus fortunei (Chinese windmill palm)

Size: reaching 20cm (8in) high by 25cm (10in) spread

Hardy waterside grass. This is a fabulous red-leaved sedge, an evergreen perennial making a dense clump of slender leaves, with white flowers in summer. Like all the sedges, a good choice for moist positions.

Uncinia rubra

FULLY HARDY

Yucca filamentosa 'Bright Edge'

Size: 2m (6½ft) tall and 1.5m (5ft) spread

Stemless and rosette-forming perennial evergreen, with variegated leaves, deep green with narrow yellow margins, which fray attractively at the edges, producing curly white threads. Readily produces panicles of white flowers, 1–2m (3–6½ft) tall, in the summer.

Yucca flaccida 'Variegata'

Size: height and spread 1.5m (5ft)

Another stemless and rosette-forming perennial evergreen, with softly drooping variegated leaves, green with bright margins. Flower panicle is 0.5 to 1m tall (1½ –3ft or so) with creamy white flowers.

Yucca gloriosa 'Variegata'

Size: 3 x 3m (9 x 9ft) eventually

Very showy and a hardy alternative to *Agave americana* 'Variegata'. This species forms a trunk, topped with a rosette of stiff, sword-like pointed leaves, green with yellow edges with age, but variegated yellow, green and pink in small specimens. It carries white flower panicles.

AGAVES

A full description of the Agave genus appears in the half-hardy section of the directory.

Size: 1–2m (3–6½ft) tall and eventual spread of 2–3m (6½–10ft)

This succulent forms rosettes of stiff, tooth-edged, blue-green leaves, with a long terminal spine. Hardy on a well-drained site in milder areas, or it can be used as an impressive house plant. Freely offsetting.

Agave americana (century plant)

Size: height 1m (3ft), eventual spread 2m (6½ft)

This is a very attractive succulent at all ages, with its long tapering rigid leaves, glossy green, with white lines and with long white fibres splitting from the edges.

Agave filifera (thread agave)

Size: height to 2m (6½ft), eventual spread 2m (6½ft) or so

This is a profusely clumping succulent species, producing rosettes of long, tapering glossy green leaves with horny margins and a long terminal spine.

Agave shawii

Size: forms a rosette up to 0.5m (1½ft) across

This succulent forms small, tightly packed rosettes with narrow pointed leaves with white markings and many fine threads on the edges. Hardy outside in Britain in a well-drained site.

Agave toumeyana

Agave univittata

Size: rosettes reach up to 1m (3ft) across

Succulent. Offsetting rosettes with long, rather thin, glossy green leaves with darker longitudinal stripes and toothed leaf edges.

Aloe striatula

Size: 1.5m (5ft) tall by about 2m (6½ft) across

Fast-growing succulent species, developing into a multi-stemmed shrub which has dark green leaves with parallel green lines on the leaf sheath. Yellow flowers on a 2m (6½ft) flower spike, carried in spring in Britain.

Aloinopsis luckhoffii

Size: Each clump is 2.5cm (1in) high with the same spread

Hardy succulent. Has thick, grey-green triangular leaves with greyish tubercles. Needs to be grown in strong light, when it will develop a reddish tint, and will remain compact. It has large, honey-scented, yellow flowers 2.5cm (1in) across in late summer.

Brahea armata (blue palm)

Size: reaches 12m (40ft) eventually

One of the most beautiful of the palms, rather like *Trachycarpus fortunei* in appearance. Beautiful shapely, stiff, blue leaves. It is slow-growing and expensive, but very desirable and looks attractive at all stages.

Size: height and spread 2m (6½ft)

This is an even choicer *Agave americana* cultivar, with a white central band down each leaf.

Agave americana 'Mediopicta Alba'

Size: height and spread 2m (6½ft)

Very attractive, half-hardy, architectural plants which look good in urns or out on patios as feature plants. They grow into huge rosettes, with long tapering green leaves splashed with yellow and cream stripes.

Agave americana 'Striata'

Size: leaves are about 25cm (10in) long

This species forms pale green rosettes with a rather shorter, more compact habit than *Agave americana*. The dark terminal spines are 3cm (over 1in) long.

Agave macrocantha

Size: 20–25cm (8–10in) diameter rosettes

These are very squat plants, with short, fat leaves up to 11cm (5in or so) wide which are an attractive pale grey-green.

Agave potatorum

HALF HARDY

HALF HARDY

Agave potatorum var. verschaffeltii

Size: 20–25cm (8–10in) diameter rosettes

Another attractive 'fat' plant, with rather shorter leaves than *Agave potatorum*.

Agave victoriae-reginae

Size: 0.6 x 0.6m (2 x 2ft)

This is a really choice agave, showing an almost artificial symmetry, with its dark green leaves striped and edged with white.

Aloe ferox (bitter aloe)

Size: reaches 2m in height (6½ft)

Single-stemmed succulents with fiercely spined grey succulent leaves. Tubular flowers on branching stalks, usually bright red, though yellow and white flowers are also known. Flowers in the spring in western Europe.

Aloe gariepensis

Size: 1m (3ft) tall

Succulent. Dark green leaves, attractively blotched white, with toothed edges. Rosettes are carried on short stems, producing 1m (3ft) flower stalks bearing masses of tubular yellow flowers, rather like those of kniphofia (red hot pokers).

Size: 1m (3ft) tall

Succulent. This is a fast-growing species in a warm position, forming stemless rosettes bearing unbranched 1m (3ft) high flower stems, with red flower buds in the spring opening to yellow flowers.

Aloe microstigma

Size: 1–2m (3–6½ft)

Succulent. A strongly offsetting species, forming a clump. With age, it topples over and becomes creeping rather than upright. It has red flowers.

Aloe mitriformis

Size: caudex up to 30cm (1ft) in diameter, leaves grow on trailing stems up to 1m (3ft)

Narrow curved leaves growing from a corky, fissured caudex (swollen root); may be hardy in milder areas.

Calibanus hookeri

HALF HARDY

Ceropegia woodii

Size: trailing stems to 1m (3ft) long

Succulent. Very attractive, grey, heart-shaped leaves with purple markings and unusual and pretty purple, lantern-shaped, flowers. Lovely choice for a half-hardy hanging basket, window box, or cascade pot.

Cleistocactus straussii

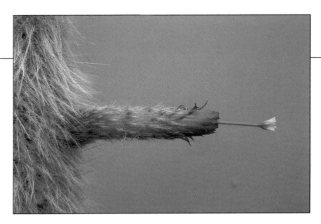

Size: grows 1m (3ft) or more

This clumping, columnar cactus is covered in a wonderful overcoat of soft white spines and bears long, almost rudimentary, scarlet flowers.

Cotyledon orbiculata

Size: grows up to 1m (3ft) tall

This succulent has a beautiful grey bloom on its fat, round leaves and carries red and yellow flowers on a long stalk. We have found that it will survive most winters if planted in a well-drained, sunny position.

Crassula pellucida subsp. *marginalis*

Size: stems up to 60cm (2ft) long

A versatile mat-forming succulent, good for edging beds and containers and for use in hanging containers. Leaves vary from green and plump in shady, wetter conditions, to smaller, maroon to purple-black in strong natural light. It has white flowers in the autumn.

Size: 1m (3ft) tall

Succulent. This is an attractive miniature tree with a distinct trunk, and many branches with fat, coin-shaped leaves and white flowers in winter. Also known as the money plant and supposed to be good feng-shui.

Crassula ovata (syn. *C. argentea/portulacea*)

Size: 1m (3ft) tall

Succulent. This is a pretty, blue leaved form of *Crassula ovata*, the money plant.

Crassula ovata (syn. *C. argentea /portulacea*) 'Blue Bird'

Size: approximately 2.5cm (1in) high, indefinite spread

Succulent. A mat-forming species which produces masses of long-lasting white flowers in summer and autumn.

Crassula cooperi

HALF HARDY

Cycas revoluta (the sago palm)

Size: 3 x 3m (9ft x 9ft) eventually, but it is slow growing so most plants in cultivation will be much smaller

Half hardy perennial. This is a choice and popular slow-growing evergreen 'palm' with an attractive trunk topped with a rosette of stiff, feathered leaves.

Dudleya farinosa

Size: up to 0.5m (20in) in diameter

Succulent. This species has rosettes of long tapering leaves with an interesting, chalky, white or grey surface and numerous red flowers borne on a tall stem.

ECHEVERIAS

Echeverias are some of the prettiest of the succulents, with beautiful cultivars in a range of pastel shades, like pinks, turquoises and lilacs, with some contrasting, much darker cultivars, ranging from dark maroons to almost black. There are also some attractive bi-colours. They make excellent summer bedding and colour up very well in natural light. They can then move indoors for winter colour in the house.

Size: rosettes are 25cm (10in) across

Impressive large, deep red to purple rosettes.

Echeveria **'Afterglow'**

Size: rosettes are 25cm (10in) across

This is a very covetable example of the dark-coloured cultivars with its red-maroon to almost black leaves. It makes a good contrast here against pale slate chippings.

Echeveria **'Black Prince'**

Size: rosettes are 15cm (6in) across

Pretty clumps of pink-lilac leaves and orange-red flowers.

Echeveria *carnicolor*

Size: rosettes are 15cm (6in) across

A tightly packed, grey-bloomed, compact rosette and yellow, orange-tinged flowers.

Echeveria *derenbergii*

HALF HARDY

HALF HARDY

Echeveria
'Easter Bonnet'

Size: rosettes are 30cm (1ft) across

Very attractive rosettes of grey-blue-green leaves with crinkled edges.

Echeveria × *fallax*

Size: rosettes are 20cm (8in) across

Attractive grey bloom. (Hybrid of *E. derenbergii* × *E. elegans.*)

Echeveria
'Filipe Otero'

Size: rosettes are 20cm (8in) across

Grey hairy leaves, with a papillose surface.

Echeveria
gibbiflora **'Carunculata'**

Size: rosettes are 0.4m (1½ft) across

Grey olive colour. Notable for the strange protuberances on the upper surface of the leaves.

Size: rosettes are 30cm (1ft) across

This has very dramatically coloured, round green leaves with bright red edges, especially when grown in full sun. The leaf edges are slightly wavy.

Echeveria **'Harry Butterfield'**

Size: rosettes are 25cm (10in) across

Slender grey leaves, streaked with cream.

Echeveria **'Hoveyii'**

Size: rosettes are 30cm (1ft) across

A vigorous grower, with bright green leaves with red edges.

Echeveria meridian

Size: rosettes are about 30cm (1ft) high and 15cm (6in) across

This is a striking, taller growing cultivar with green leaves, which have strongly contrasting red and brown streaks and patches all over them.

Echeveria nodulosa **'Painted Beauty'**

HALF HARDY

Echeveria 'Painted Frills'

Size: rosettes are 30cm (1ft)

Very pretty rosettes of wavy red, brown and olive green leaves.

Echeveria pilosa × harmsii

Size: forms clumps to 60cm (2ft) across and 30cm (1ft) high

Another taller-growing cultivar, branching with papillose stems.

Echeveria ramilette

Size: rosettes are at least 30cm (1ft) across

A large, dull green, freely offsetting species. Yellow flowers.

Echeveria 'Red Edge'

Size: rosettes are 20cm (8in) across

Very attractive large rosettes of rounded to slightly wavy leaves, coloured green and marked with red lines and patches, and with very bright red edges. It has a very stout flower spike.

Size: rosettes are 23cm (9in) across

Pretty blue-grey species with orange and yellow flowers.

Echeveria secunda

Size: rosettes are 30cm (1ft) across

A very unusual plant and one of the best echeverias, with attractive green-grey leaves covered with a 'down' of dense white hairs.

Echeveria setosa

Size: rosettes are 60cm (2ft) across

A large and exceptionally pretty grey-blue species.

Echeveria subrigida

Size: rosettes are 20cm (8in) across

Rosettes of blue-grey leaves with red edges.

Echeveria subsessilis

HALF HARDY

Euphorbia cooperi

Size: over 5m (16ft) tall in habitat, so will make 1–2m (3–6½ft) in cultivation

Succulent. This is a fast-growing, much-branching cactus look-alike (it is an example of parallel evolution in the old and new worlds). It has spiny green, multi-angled, branches.

Euphorbia fasciculata

Size: 0.5m (20in) tall

Succulent. Branching, spiny green columns with rudimentary leaves. Small yellow flowers on long stalks.

Euphorbia myrsinites

Size: stems up to 30cm (1ft) tall

Succulent. Grey-green stems arranged in spirals, with 4cm (almost 2in) long leaves. Has a yellow inflorescence.

Furcraea selloa var. marginata

Size: 1.5m (5ft) tall

Succulent. Has a stiff rosette of sword-like leaves, green-edged with yellow margins, topping a solitary trunk.

Size: 30cm (1ft)

Unusual green tongue-like leaves with cream stripes.

Gasteria
(variegated cultivar)

Size: 0.45 x 0.45m (1½ x 1½ft)

Succulent. Similar to echeveria, this plant has succulent leaves with an attractive purplish-grey bloom; its filigree-like flower stalks remain on the plant as a decorative feature for months.

Graptopetalum pentandrum
subsp. *superbum*

Size: 20cm (8in) tall and 30cm (1ft) in diameter

Succulent. This cultivar has thick, oval leaves covered in a red-grey bloom and arranged in a rosette.

Graptoveria
'Opalina'

Size: indefinite spread, a clump will reach 30cm (1ft) in diameter and 15cm (6in) tall in a year

Succulent. Clumping plant, with dark green windowed leaves with lighter markings. It has small white flowers on a long slender stalk.

Haworthia mirabilis
subsp. *mundula*

HALF HARDY

Kalanchoe
'Mirabella'

Size: indefinite size, after one year it will be 30cm (1ft) wide and 1m (3ft) long. Flowers 2cm (¾in) long

Half-hardy trailing subject with profuse orange-red flowers. Flowers in late spring; these last for a long time. Very tolerant of wet and dry conditions. Good for a low-maintenance hanging basket or window box in the summer.

Kalanchoe
tubiflora

Size: erect stems to 1m (3ft) tall

Young plants are formed on the leaf tips, drop off and quickly root. Cylindrical leaves with reddish dots. Kids love the novelty of these tiny 'plantlings'.

LITHOPS (living stones)

Lithops are to be found growing half-submerged in very dry areas of southern Africa. They strongly resemble spotted and mottled pebbles, hence their popular name. With age they form fine clusters. Their large, daisy-like flowers, often produced when the plants are quite small, are either white or yellow. They are autumn flowering.

Lithops
localis

Size: 1–2cm across (under 1 inch)

Succulent. Clump-forming, with dotted leaves and yellow flowers.

Size: shrub about 1m (3ft) tall

Cactus. Shrubby, sometimes with a short stem, and quite branching. It has lightly spined oval pads, and it readily produces its sulphur yellow 4cm (1½in) diameter flowers.

Opuntia jamaicensis

Size: 3–4m (9–13ft or so)

Cactus. A fast-growing species which forms a trunk a few metres tall and has velvety grey-green pads with attractive spines and large yellow flowers. It will stand a few degrees of frost.

Opuntia leucotricha

Size: 2–4m (6½–13ft) tall

Cactus. Rapidly growing, dark green, clustering columns which can be ruthlessly beheaded to make candelabrum-shaped plants.

Opuntia subulata

HALF HARDY

HALF HARDY

Oscularia caulescens

Size: 2cm (almost 1in) high, indefinite spread

Succulent. Low growing and spreading, with grey-green leaves and masses of pink flowers.

Pelargonium carnosum

Size: up to 30cm (1ft) tall

Caudiciform. This is a succulent geranium, with swollen, branching stems, often twisted or gnarled, up to 5cm (2in) thick which makes it a good mock-bonsai plant. It has aromatic foliage and carries numerous whitish flowers.

Sedum cauticola

Size: 12cm (5in) tall stems

Succulent. Forms a mat of semi-erect grey leaves, spotted with purple, and bearing attractive lilac flowers.

Sedum morganianum (donkey's or burro's tails)

Size: pendant stems, reaching 30cm (1ft) long with an indefinite spread

Succulent. Beautiful grey-green, trailing plant. One of the best choices for an easy-care hanging basket, summer window box or, as here, in a strawberry pot.

Size: long branching stems up to 1m (3ft)

Succulent. Good in hanging baskets and window boxes. Vibrant orange leaves, which colour up especially well in strong sun, Fragrant white flowers.

Sedum nussbaumerianum

Size: trailing stems up to 1m (3ft) long

Succulent. This is a trailing plant with bright green bead-like leaves, 8mm ($\frac{1}{3}$ in) in diameter, which makes an interesting display in a hanging basket.

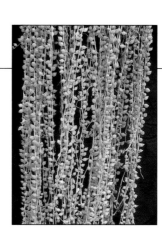

Senecio rowleyanus (string of beads)

HALF HARDY

FROST-RESISTANT CACTI & SUCCULENTS

ALL OF THESE CHOICES HAVE BEEN REPORTED TO BE COLD HARDY AND FROST RESISTANT.

TRUE CACTI

Austrocactus
bertinii
coxii
hibernus
patagonicus
spiniflorus

Coryphantha
echinus
sulcata

Echinocereus
chloranthus
chloranthus var. *russanthus*
engelmannii
engelmannii var. *chrysocentrus*
englemannii var. *purpureus*

englemannii var. *variegatus*
fasciculatus
fendleri and var. *bonkerae*
fendleri and var. *ledingii*
oklahomensis (syn. *reichenbachii*)
pectinatus
pectinatus var. *dasyacanthus*
pentalophus
reichenbachii
reichenbachii var. *baileyi*
reichenbachii var. *caespitosus*
reichenbachii var. *castaneus*
reichenbachii var. *perbellus*
triglochidiatus
triglochidiatus var. *gonacanthus*
triglochidiatus var. *gurneyi*
triglochidiatus var. *inermis*
triglochidiatus var.
  melanacanthus
viridiflorus

Echinomastus
johnsonii

Escobaria (Neobessaya)
dasyacantha
hesteri
leei
minima
missouriensis
organensis
sneedii
villardii
vivipara var. *arizonica*
vivipara var. *kaibabensis*
vivipara var. *neomexicana*
and others

Gymnocalycium
bruchii
gibbosum

Maihuenia
  patagonica
  poeppegii

Maihueniopsis (syn. Opuntia)
  darwinii

Mammillaria
  meiacantha
  wrightii

Opuntia
  acanthocarpa
  acanthocarpa var. *coloradensis*
  arbuscula
  arenaria
  atrispina
  basilaris
  basilaris var. *aurea*
  basilaris var. *cordata*
  bulbispina
  chlorotica
  clavata
  compressa (syn. *rafinesque,*
  humifusa)
  drummondii
  echinocarpa
  engelmannii
  erinacea (and varieties)
  fragilis
  fragilis var. *brachyarthra*
    humifusa (syn. *compressa*)
  hystricina
  kleiniae
  leptocaulis
  lindheimerii
  lindheimerii var. *linguiformis*
  mackensenii
  macrocentra (and forms of
    violaceae)

  macrorhiza
  martiniana (syn. *litoralis*
    martiniana)
  nicholii (var. of *hystricina*)
  penicilligera
  phaeacantha
  polyacantha
  pulchella
  pusilla
  rubiflora
  santa-rita (form of *violacea*)
  schweriniana
  sphaerocarpa
  spinosior
  sulphurea
  tortispina
  tortispina var. *cymochila*
  tunicata var. *davisii*
  violacea
  viridiflora
  whipplei

Pediocactus
  simpsonii
  and all other species

Pterocactus
  araucanus
  australis
  fischeri
  hickenii
  kuntzei
  valentinii

Sclerocactus (syn. Thelocactus)
  possibly

OTHER SUCCULENTS

Agave
  havardiana
  lecheguilla
  murpheyii
  mckelvyana
  palmeri
  palmeri var. *chrysantha*
  parryi
  parviflora
  toumeyana
  utahensis var. *eborispina*
  utahensis var. *kaibabensis*
  utahensis var. *nevadensis*

Aloe
  aristata
  broomii
  polyphylla

Aloinopsis (Titanopsis)
  hilmari
  luckhoffii
  malherbei
  orpenii
  peersii
  rosulata
  rubrolineata
  schoonesii
  setifera
  thudichumii
  villettii

Anacampseros
  crinita

Bulbine
  frutescens

Caralluma
  europaea var. *confusa*
  munbyana var. *hispanica*

Chasmatophyllum
  muscolinum

Chiastophyllum
  oppositifolium

Cotyledon
  orbiculata
  simulans

Crassula
  alba
  capitella
  corallina
  dependens
  natalensis
  nudicaullis
  sarcocaulis
  sarcocaulis subsp. *rupicola*
  setulosa

Dasylirion
  wheeleri

Delosperma
  aberdeenense
  ashtonii
  brunnthaleri
  clavipes
  concavum
  congestum
  cooperi
  hirtum
  incomptum
  incomptum var. *gracile*

  kofleri
  lavisiae
  lavisiae var. *parisepalum*
  lineare
  mahonii
  nelii
  nubigenum
  obtusum
  roseopurpureum
  sutherlandii

Drosanthemum
  floribundum

Euphorbia
  mysinites

Herroa
  herrei
  incurva
  muirii
  wilmaniae

Hesperaloe
  parviflora

Huernia
  barbata
  confusa

Jovibarba
  heuffelii

Lewisia
  brachycalyx
  cotyledon
  nevadensis
  pygmaea
  rediviva

Lithops
  most are said to be hardy
  to –10˚C (14˚F) if kept dry

Malephora
  crocea
  lutea

Mestoklema
  arboriforme
  tuberosum

Nananthus (Aloinopsis)
  transvaalensis
  wilmaniae

Neohenricia
  sibbettii

Orostachys
  boehmeri
  iwarenge
  minutus
  spinosa

Rabiea
  possibly all but certainly
  albinota

Rhinephyllum
  broomii
  muirii
  schonlandii

Rhombophyllum
  dolabriforme

Rosularia
  most

Ruschia
  hamata
  pulvinaris
  putterilii
  uncinata

Sedum
  many

Sempervivella
  most

Sempervivum
  most

Sphalmanthus
  several including *resurgens*

Stapelia
  some clones may be hardy
  ambigua
  flavirostris
  grandiflora
  (are all now usually grouped
  under grandiflora)

Stomatium
  the more toothed types including
  fulleri
  patulum
  peersii
  suaveolens

Talinum
  okanoganense

Titanopsis
  calcarea
  fulleri

Toumeya
  papyracantha

Trichodiadema
  these will die down to the
  ground in winter but resprout in
  the spring

Yucca
  aloifolia
  angustissima
  angustissima subsp. *avia*
  angustissima subsp. *kanabensis*
  angustissima subsp. *toftiae*
  arkansana
  baccata
  baccata subsp. *vespertina*
  baileyii
  baileyii subsp. *intermedia*
  brevifolia (Joshua Tree)
  campestris
  carnerosana
  constricta
  elata
  elata (syn. *glauca* var. *radiosa*)
  elata subsp. *utahensis*
  elata subsp. *verdiensis*
  faxonia
  filamentosa
  filifera
  flaccida (syn. *filamentosa* var.
    flaccida)
  glauca
  glauca var. *intermedia (syn.*
    Yucca baileyii subsp. *intermedia)*
  glauca var. *gurneyi* (syn. *Yucca*
    glauca subsp. *stricta*)
  glauca var. *mollis* (syn. *Yucca*
    arkansana)
  gloriosa

  gloriosa 'Variegata'
  harrimaniae
  harrimaniae subsp. *neomexicana*
  harrimaniae subsp. *sterilis*
  louisianenesis
  nana
  pallida
  recurvifolia
  reverchonii
  rigida
  rostrata
  rupicola
  schidigera
  schottii
  thompsoniana
  torreyi
  treculeana
  whipplei

Glossary

Accent planting – a particularly large and dramatic plant or plants, used as the most important feature in a scheme

Acid soil – soil that has a pH value of less than 7

Aerial roots – these appear from the stem of the plant, above soil level

Alpines – strictly speaking plants that have originated in the high mountains, above the tree line, but used as a loose general term for all rockery plants

Annual bedding – a scheme using plants that complete their whole life cycle in one year

Annuals – plants that complete their whole life cycle from germination, flowering and seeding to death in one year

Areole – of cacti, the portion of the plant from which the spines originate

Architectural – in the sense of plants, refers to plants that have a particularly strong shape and form

Aromatic – scented, usually in the sense of fragrant herbs

Basal rosette – leaves radiating from a central point at ground level

Bi-colours – flowers that have two contrasting shades

Biennial – plants that complete their whole life cycle from germination, flowering and seeding to death in two years; producing roots, stems and leaves in the first year, and flowering, seeding and dying in the second year

Bloom (see also Felt) – blue or greyish fine, waxy or powdery coating on leaves or stems

Bonsai-like succulents – tree-like succulents, which make instant or almost instant, miniature trees for growing in pots

Border – cultivated area, edging e.g. lawns, patios etc.

Borderline hardy – will survive in an average to warmer than average British winter, but which will be cut down by severe and prolonged frosts

Borrowed heat – heat which escapes from intentionally warmed spaces into unheated adjacent spaces; e.g. a unheated conservatory, which will remain warmer than a freestanding structure because of the escape of heat into it through the house walls.

Bract – a modified leaf, which is produced at the base of a flower, or a flower cluster. They are often large and brightly coloured

Bromeliad – erect or semi-prostrate evergreen rosette-forming plants with stiff foliage

Butting – putting two surfaces together as closely as possible without overlapping them.

Cactus – a member of the Cactaceae family, usually highly succulent, with spines produced from areoles

Candelabrum (of plants) – a plant with a number of branching arms

Carpet bedding – low-growing, mat-forming and often succulent plants which can be used in a tapestry-effect planting scheme

Carpeting succulents – succulents suitable for use in carpet bedding schemes

Columnar (of plants) – upright habit of growth, forming tall cylindrical structures

Combination planting – in the context of this book, the use of drought-resistant and/or architectural plants in schemes alongside more traditional herbaceous planting schemes.

Conifer – cone-bearing and evergreen tree or shrub

Container plant – plant suitable for growing in moveable pots

Continental climate – characterized by the hot summers, cold winters and low rainfall typical of conditions in the interior of a continent away from the sea

Cordon – horticulturally, this involves removing all projecting branches, and training side branches from a central trunk along wires or similar to create a completely flat, wall-like structure

Corona – a crown-shaped or cup-like feature of a flower, between the petals and the stamens

Cultivar – an artificially produced plant, either bred or selected, which can be propagated while retaining its characteristics.

Cylindrical (of plants) – see columnar

Debud/disbud – remove buds to prevent flowering

Deciduous – describes plants that produce fresh leaves annually at the beginning of the growing season, and lose them when the growing season comes to an end

Decking – structure of wooden planking, for terraces, patios and other areas of hard landscaping

Desiccated – dehydrated and dried up

Drought resistant – able to tolerate periods without water

Dwarf – a shorter form of a plant

Elliptical – shaped like a flattened circle, like a rugby ball

Ericaceous (of compost) – acidic, and therefore suitable for acid-loving plants

Etiolated – long spindly pale growth in plants, which results from too little light

Evergreen – has leaves all the year round; though leaves do die and are replaced this is a continuous process and therefore unnoticeable

Exclamation plants – see accent planting

Exotic (of gardens) – non-native and unexpected, usually originating in much hotter areas

Felt – (see Bloom)

Filigree-like – delicate, interlacing habit, resembling the fine, lace-like patterns in twisted silver and gold jewellery

Flexible surfacing (of hard landscaping) – involves loose-laid surfaces, which can be removed and changed

Focal planting – the most visually important plants in a scheme, placed to draw the most possible attention

Focal point – the area where focal planting has been used, or where there is an eye-catching container, statue, water feature etc.

Frost pocket – a purely localized area, which, because of geographical features, is significantly colder in winter than the surrounding areas

Fully hardy – a plant which can tolerate temperatures of down to ‾15°C (5°F)

Genus – a group of species that share enough common characteristics to be grouped together for the purpose of botanical identification

Globular (of plants) – having a spherical or ball-like shape

Gravel bed – a particular style of planting, involving the use of a bed with a surface dressing of gravel

Ground cover – carpeting and mat-forming species that rapidly cover bare areas

Habitat – original geographical area where the plants grow wild

Half hardy – plants which can only go outside after any danger of frost has passed and which have to come indoors for the winter before frosts are likely

Hard core – material, such as broken bricks and rocks, which acts as a compacted foundation layer for a surface material like gravel or paving slabs

Hard landscaping – structures in the garden like paths, steps, patios etc.

Hardiness zones – see Harvard University hardiness zones

Harvard University hardiness zones – a system developed in the USA by Harvard University in which areas are a rated according to the temperature requirements of the plants that they can support

Herbaceous – plants which die down at the end of the growing season

High maintenance – a scheme that will demand a great deal of time and attention

Honey fungus – a rapidly spreading fungal infection which sometimes develops on dead trees and branches

Hybrid – offspring of at least two different species or varieties or plant, which can be naturally or artificially produced

Infilling – temporary planting to fill in a bed or border until the permanent planting matures sufficiently to fill the space

Inflorescence – a flowering shoot, which carries more than one flower

Insecticide – a toxic substance for destroying insect pests

Invasive – plants which can quickly outgrow their space and/or overwhelm their neighbours

Island bed – an isolated planting area, designed to be viewed from all sides, in the round

Knot garden – a formal garden, comprising regular beds planted on a geometrical pattern, divided by low hedging, like box (*Buxus sempervirens*)

Low maintenance – easy-care planting schemes requiring the minimum of attention

Marginal – a moisture-loving species, which enjoys a damp position on the edges of a pond or other water feature

Maritime climate – a climate affected by proximity to the sea, which results in a relatively small temperature difference between the summer and winter months and fairly high rainfall

Metabolic rate – the speed with which all the chemical processes of a living body take place

Microclimate – a climate that is particular to a very small area and affected by local factors, e.g. the higher temperatures found in a city environment because of the combination of shelter created by buildings and the extra heat resulting from the escape of energy from densely packed habitation, industry etc.

Mid-stripe – a central band of contrasting colour in a leaf or flower petal

Mulch – a layer of material added to the soil surface to protect plants, suppress weeds and retain moisture

Non-invasive – a plant that will not outgrow its position or affect neighbouring plants

Offsetting – a plant which produces miniature replicas of itself, usually around its base

Outcrop – a rock formation that is visible on the surface

Panicles – a branched flower cluster

Papillose – covered in minute, blunt projections

Pergola – horizontal trellis or frame, supported on pillars or posts, used for climbing plants

Permeable membrane – this is a layer of material designed to be placed between the surface of the soil and a top dressing of gravel; it suppresses weeds and light while allowing air and water to pass through it

Plumes – feather-like heads

Prick out – transplanting seedlings or young plants which are becoming crowded into another container to give them more space to grow

Propagate – to produce extra plants by setting seeds, taking cuttings, grafting etc.

Propagator – a container, with heat and/or light, which gives seeds, cuttings etc. the best possible conditions for maximum growth

Prostrate – a sprawling, low-growing habit

Racemes – unbranched flower clusters

Rhizome – underground creeping stem, which functions as a storage organ and produces leaves and shoots

Rigid surfacing – hard landscaping involving the construction of a solid, immoveable slab; e.g. as in laying concrete paths and patios

Riven paving – paving slabs made of artificial stone with an impressed pattern which suggests that the stone has actually been split from a rock face – to give a more sympathetic and textured surface and to improve grip

Rosette-shaped – a group of leaves which radiate from a central point

Rule of 3 or 5 – the fact that irregular numbers of plants of the same species create a more natural look, by blending irregularly into adjacent planting

Scree bed – a bed which shows gradation from large rocks, through cobbles to smaller pebbles, to suggest a natural rockfall

Screening – using plants or materials like trellis to hide parts of the garden which are unsightly, to give shelter, to divide planting areas etc.

Shrubs – woody stemmed plants, often much branching

Sleepers – large rectangular blocks of wood, as used in railway track. They provide large and virtually indestructible material for edging beds, and they are used to construct decking foundations, steps, etc.

Sour soil – soil that has become starved of nutrients or has an undesirable build up of chemicals

Spathe – a hood-shaped bract around a spike-shaped inflorescence

Species – a member of a genus

Specimen plant – a large or particularly exotic plant that is displayed in splendid isolation to reveal its beauty, form, etc.

Spines/spination – a hard outgrowth from a stem; in cacti they are an evolutionary modification of leaves

Stemless – a plant that lacks a main ascending axis; see basal rosettes

Strata – the distinct layers laid down during the formation of sedimentary rock

Stratified rockery – a rockery in which the stones are laid in an imitation of the way that a rock outcrop would have formed naturally

Subspecies – members of a species, which share common features within themselves that separate them from the rest of the species

Succulent/ence (of plants) – a plant that has evolved to withstand periods of drought, by modifying the leaves, stems or roots for improved water storage

Suckering – plants which produce extra growth from below the ground by producing shoots from the original rootstock

Summer bedding – see half-hardy bedding

Systemic insecticide – a longer-lasting chemical taken up into the whole of the plant so that it continues to poison insects which feed on it; as opposed to a non-systemic insecticide, which coats the outside of the plant and insects temporarily but is soon washed away

Temperate climate/zone – a moderate or mild climate; areas which have such a climate

Thickets – a dense growth of small trees, shrubs or similar

Topiary – trees or bushes, which have been trained and clipped into artificial shapes – e.g. geometrical or animal shapes

Trailing – a plant with long stems which hang down; particularly useful for baskets, window boxes etc.

Variegation – foliage that displays lighter banding, striping or spotting

Water table – the point at which you reach the water-saturated layer under the surface of the soil

Winter protection – a layer of protective material, like horticultural fleece, sacking, straw or even the plant's own foliage, which is used to cover the plant over the winter. The protected plant can then stay outside happily all winter.

Woody (stems) – a persistent stem of woody fibres, which means that the plant does not die down over the winter as herbaceous material does

Further reading

Cacti for the Connoisseur, by John Pilbeam, B T Batsford, 1987
This is the book for a definitive list of currently accepted names – there have been many changes over the years.

Cacti, the Illustrated Dictionary, by Rod and Ken Preston-Mafham, Cassell, 1998 (first published 1991 by Blandford)
A huge photographic guide to the globular cacti, over 1,000 species presented in colour photographs alphabetically arranged, along with brief descriptions of the plants and invaluable details of alternative names.

Glossary of Botanical Terms with special reference to Succulent Plants, compiled by Urs Eggli, published by the British Cactus and Succulent Society, 1993
This is a really useful alphabetical dictionary of botanical terms with several pages of line drawings explaining terms for leaf and flower shapes, etc.

Guide to the Aloes of South Africa, by Ben-Erik Van Wyk and Gideon Smith, Briza, 1996
More than 400 colour photographs, showing plants in habitat and close ups of leaves and flowers, this book features plant descriptions of the 125 species of the region, split into groups based on habit of growth, with helpful distribution maps. It also deals with related aloe-like plants, like agaves, gasterias etc., medicinal and cosmetic uses, conservation issues etc.

Lithops – Treasures of the Veld, by Steven Hammer, British Cactus and Succulent Society, 1999
Invaluable identifier with 225 colour photographs, 10 line drawings, 2 maps.

Mesembryanthemums of the World, an Illustrated Guide to a Remarkable Succulent Group; written by nine respected botanical experts, Briza, 1998
405 pages, and lavishly illustrated with over 800 colour photographs, this book is for the enthusiast who wants to know more about these diverse and beautiful plants.

Sedum, Cultivated Stonecrops, by Ray Stephenson, Timber Press, 1994
Ray Stephenson holds the National Collection of Sedums at his home in the north of England. This book describes over 400 species and varieties, with advice on care, cultivation and propagation, and habitat information. 356 pages, with 110 colour photographs and 100 black and white photographs.

The Cactus Handbook, by Tony Sato, Japan Cactus Planning Press, 1996
345 pages and 3,006 excellent colour photographs.

This is a wonderful picture book for the enthusiast, an excellent plant identifier, written in Japanese and English with correct botanical names under each colour photograph.

The Hillier Manual of Trees and Shrubs, pocket edition, David & Charles, first published 1972, latest edition 1998
A useful dictionary of descriptions (no pictures).

The Royal Horticultural Society New Encyclopaedia of Plants & Flowers, Editor in Chief, Christopher Brickell, Dorling Kindersley, 3rd edition 1999
Over 8,000 plants and 4,250 photographs, covering everything the gardener could be looking for (or looking at without knowing it!).

Succulents, the Illustrated Dictionary, by Maurizio Sajeva and Mariengela Constanzo, Cassell, 1994, last reprint 1998
This is the companion volume to the Preston-Mafham *Cacti, the Illustrated Dictionary*, but dealing with the 'other' succulents. Includes more than 1,200 photographs of species and varieties from 195 different genera.

Succulents II, the New Illustrated Dictionary, by Maurizio Sajeva and Mariangela Constanzo, Timber Press, 2000
This has the same layout as *Succulents*, above. *Succulents II* has more than 1,200 colour photographs and includes more than 900 species not illustrated in the first book. Every species illustrated is described with information on shape, size, colour and growth form, plus country of origin and CITES status. Introductory chapters cover habitat and genera information plus cultivation details.

The following are out of print, sadly, but are worth looking out for in libraries or second-hand bookshops:

The Cactus Handbook, by Erik Haustein, Cathay Books, 1988
Useful encyclopaedia covering columnar as well as globular cacti, but most useful for its readable introduction to all the botany you would ever need to know for cactus collecting.

The Illustrated Encyclopaedia of Cacti, by Clive Innes and Charles Glass, Headline, 1991
Illustrates and identifies over 1,200 species, including columnar and epiphytic cacti as well as just the globular species.

The Illustrated Encyclopaedia of Succulents, Gordon Rowley, Salamander Books, 1978
Covers cacti and succulents, crammed full of pictures. The author had a wonderful, anecdotal and therefore very readable style.

Further information

British Cactus and Succulent Society (BCSS)
The objectives of the Society are to promote the study, conservation, propagation and cultivation of cacti and other succulent plants. Membership of the Society is open to all. Affiliated to The Royal Horticultural Society, the BCSS was formed in 1983 by the amalgamation of the two major cactus and succulent societies in the UK, The National Cactus and Succulent Society (NCSS) and The Cactus and Succulent Society of Great Britain (CSSGB), both of which had long histories. Membership of the BCSS is currently about 3,800 and includes novice window-sill growers to experts. The Society has just under 100 branches in the UK which organize an active programme of events every year. As well as holding local meetings, shows and producing an information-packed quarterly magazine, the Society has several Round Robin groups on a number of topics. Group members share ideas and information, and one of the Robins deals specifically with cold-hardy cacti and succulents. For more information and membership enquiries contact the Membership Secretary: D V Slade, 15 Brentwood Crescent, Hull Road, York, Y010 5HU. Tel: 01904 410512, website: http://www.bcss.org.uk.

The Cactus and Succulent Plant Mall (CSPM)
A fabulous resource full of links and information to the world of cacti and other succulents. Website: http://www.cactus-mall.com. The site is regularly updated with information on cactus and succulent societies and suppliers of plants, seeds and literature. The CSPM has developed and hosts web pages for more than 100 cactus and succulent organizations worldwide. It also aims to maintain as complete a list of web pages and other cactus- and succulent-related Internet facilities as possible. The CSPM is maintained by Suzanne and Tony Mace who will be pleased to receive comments or additional material for inclusion. The CSPM includes the official web pages for the three largest cactus and succulent societies in the world – American, British and German – plus other important ones such as the South African and Mexican societies.

The Amateurs' Digest
A fabulous website at www.TheAmateursDigest.com. Offers loads of information on line plus links to other succulents sites. Or e-mail them on amatrdigest@coastnet.com.

The Amateurs' Digest
Edited by Marina Welham, this bi-monthly publication is written and illustrated by lovers of succulent plants. It deals with cacti, succulents, caudiciforms and other collectables. This is a friendly and helpful publication, with a welcoming manner and jam-packed with interesting features. For more information and subscriptions contact: Marina Welham, The Amateurs' Digest, Dept. G, 8591 Lochside Drive, Sidney, BC, V8L IM5, Canada.

David Sierer and The (Not) Too Cold For Cactus Group
A really interesting discussion group and website that can be reached via The Amateurs' Digest website listed above.

The Hardy Cacti Group
An e-mail community sharing experiences of growing cacti and other succulents outside. E-mail them on: listproc@opus.labs.agilent.com to receive e-mail digest 'HardyCactietc.Digest'.

Society of Garden Designers
For details of approved garden designers, you can contact the Society of Garden Designers (affiliated to the Royal Horticultural Society) at the Institute of Horticulture, 14/15 Belgrave Square, London, SW1X 8PS. Tel: 0207 838 9311.

British Association of Landscape Industries (BALI)
BALI at Landscape House. Stoneleigh Park, Warwickshire, CV8 2LG. Tel: 02746 690333 can recommend accredited garden landscaping companies – it takes two years for an organization to gain accreditation.

InstaPlant®
Developed by Kernock Park Plants and specializing in succulents, the InstaPlant® system works by using computer-aided technology to convert carpet bedding ideas into displays, from small private beds to large corporate or municipal schemes. On delivery the customer simply slides pre-rooted tiles of plants out of their trays according to a set plan, onto a pre-prepared bed. This means the bed instantly becomes a colourful work of art within hours, making light work of a previously labour-intensive task. For further information and quotations contact Kernock Park Plants, Pillaton. Saltash, Cornwall PL12 6RY. Tel: 01579 350561, fax: 01579 351151, e-mail: enquiries@kernock.co.uk, website: www.kernock.co.uk.

About the author

Since 1977, Shirley-Anne Bell has been building up her own retail and mail-order plant business, Glenhirst Cactus Nursery, in Lincolnshire, East Midlands, England, with the assistance of her photographer husband, Neville. While raising their three children, Shirley-Anne gained a first-class honours degree with the Open University in History of Art, Architecture and Design, and English. During the 1980s her poetry was widely published and she was a writer in residence, ran writing workshops, gave national readings, was a literature consultant for Lincolnshire and Humberside Arts, and edited *Proof*, the regional literary magazine.

This is Shirley-Anne's first published book on cacti and other succulents, though she has already written her second on growing cacti and other succulents in the conservatory and indoors, which will be published by GMC Publications later in 2001. She is also a regular contributor to GMC's *Exotic Gardening* magazine. The Nursery publishes its own catalogues and guides and has a vast picture library, including pictures taken on travels to cacti- and succulent-inhabited countries overseas.

To speak to Shirley-Anne and for more information contact:
Glenhirst Cactus Nursery, Station Road, Swineshead, Near Boston, Lincolnshire PE20 3NX. Tel: 01205 820314, fax: 01205 820614, e-mail: sabell@glenhirstcactiandpalms.co.uk, website: www.glenhirstcactiandpalms.co.uk.

Index